Company's Coming

Gifts from the Kitchen

Photo Legend front and back covers:

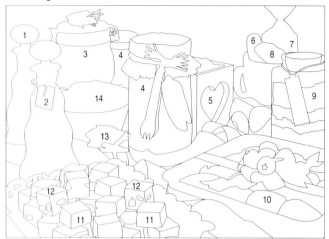

Gifts from the Kitchen

Eighth Printing June 2006

Library and Archives Canada Cataloguing in Publication
Paré, Jean, date
Company's Coming, Gifts from the kitchen
(Special occasion series)
Includes index.
ISBN 1-895455-69-3
1. Cookery. 2. Gifts. I. Title. II. Series: Paré, Jean, Special occasion series.
TX714.P356 2001   641.5   C2001-900445-1

Published by
Company's Coming Publishing Limited
2311 – 96 Street
Edmonton, Alberta, Canada T6N 1G3
Tel: 780-450-6223   Fax: 780-450-1857
www.companyscoming.com

Company's Coming is a registered trademark owned by Company's Coming Publishing Limited

Colour separations by Friesens, Altona, Manitoba, Canada
Printed in China

Pictured at left:
Top Left: Strawberry Divinity, page 57
Top Right: Coffee Fudge, page 57
Bottom Right: Truffles, page 56

Gifts from the Kitchen was created thanks to the dedicated efforts of the people and organizations listed below.

COMPANY'S COMING PUBLISHING LIMITED

Author	Jean Paré
President	Grant Lovig
Vice President, Product Development	Kathy Knowles
Design Manager	Derrick Sorochan
Senior Designer	Jaclyn Draker
Publishing Coordinator	Shelly Willsey
Copy Editor	Debbie Dixon

The Recipe Factory

Research & Development Manager	Nora Prokop
Editor	Laurel Hoffmann
Editorial Assistant	Rendi Dennis
Proofreaders	Audrey Dahl
	Audrey Whitson
Food Editor	Lynda Elsenheimer
Associate Food Editor	Suzanne Hartman
Researcher	Betty Chase
Test Kitchen Coordinator	Allison Dosman
Test Kitchen Staff	Ellen Bunjevac
	Janice Ciesielski
	Pat Yukes
Photography Coordinator	Karen Decoux
Photographer	Stephe Tate Photo
Senior Food Stylist	Sherri Cunningham
Food Stylist	Francine Allan
Prep Kitchen Staff	Shannon Durocher
	Dana Royer
	Audrey Smetaniuk
Prop Stylists	Paula Bertamini
	Snezana Ferenac
Nutrition Analyst	Margaret Ng, B.Sc., M.A., R.D.

Our special thanks to the following businesses for providing extensive props for photography.

A Taste Of Provence	Pier 1 Imports
Anchor Hocking Canada	Popcorn Plus
Artifacts	Pyrex® Bakeware
Bernardin Ltd.	Pyrex® Portables
Browne & Co. Ltd.	Stokes
Canadian Tire	The Bay
Crafts Canada	The Plaid Giraffe
Cuisipro	Treasure Barrel
Dansk Gifts	Via
Linens 'N Things	Wal-Mart Canada Inc.
London Drugs	Winners Stores
Michael's The Arts And Crafts Store	Zellers

Foreword

Homemade pies brimming with fresh fruit and crumbling with light pastry. Chocolaty brownies that melt in your mouth. A jar of pickles that pucker your lips. These goodies and more await you in *Gifts from the Kitchen*, to make and share with friends and family.

In an age where "I'm too busy" is often heard, it might be fun to slow down long enough to create something unique and personal. With ideas from *Gifts from the Kitchen*, you can make any food look special, for any occasion or event.

The section on Gift-Giving Etiquette helps you navigate through the confusion of what to give and when. There are even tips on how to get your casserole dishes returned (if you don't intend to give the dish as part of the gift)!

Surprise your brother with Bottoms-Up Pizza for his birthday, or spoil Mom by giving her Truffles on Mother's Day. Bake Mud Cake for a thoughtful friend— just because—or for a teacher who helped your child this past year. And that college student who's always calling home would probably appreciate a care package of cookies and a ready-to-make soup mix.

Gifts from the Kitchen has ideas for holidays and housewarmings, plus recipes to make for loved ones in times of hardship. Whether you know someone who just got a promotion or who is bringing home a new baby, these pages are packed with recipes they'll enjoy. Even if you know people who don't appreciate a plateful of cookies, we've also covered that with the section on Gifts for the Home. Make up some tubs of play dough or finger paints for children, or create home decorations out of dried herbs. Or pamper someone who needs to relax with a gift of bath luxuries.

Every recipe is not only featured in full-color but is also shown gifted to help stimulate your imagination for ideas on how to dress up a gift with bags, boxes, labels and ribbons. Make a beautiful and easy bow to decorate a box, shrink-wrap a basket of homemade goodies, or turn a place mat into a casserole holder with our simple instructions.

With *Gifts from the Kitchen*, it truly is better to give than to receive because of how good you feel when you can say, "I made that!"

Jean Paré

Each recipe has been analyzed using the most up-to-date version of the Canadian Nutrient File from Health Canada, which is based on the United States Department of Agriculture (USDA) Nutrient Database. If more than one ingredient is listed (such as "hard margarine or butter"), then the first ingredient is used in the analysis. Where an ingredient reads "sprinkle," "optional," or "for garnish," it is not included as part of the nutrition information.

Margaret Ng, B.Sc. (Hon), M.A.
Registered Dietitian

Table of Contents

Gift-Giving Etiquette

Creating a gift from the kitchen is not necessarily less expensive than purchasing something from a store. But an item you took the time and effort to pull together is what will strike family and friends as thoughtful, because it is unique!

As the saying goes, "It's the thought that counts." When you consider giving a gift, think about the reason and whether it reflects the receiver's tastes. Think of their hobbies, interests or job. For example, a person on a diet would prefer a gift for the home rather than chocolates. Steer clear of giving scented items to people with a sensitive nose. Consider quantity when you're making something. Don't give a couple something that serves ten and, likewise, don't prepare a small box of candy for a family of six. When making gifts for children, make sure the gifts are age appropriate. A box of finger paints is just right for ages 4 to 8, while older children may prefer a container of snacks.

Take a few moments to label, tie, decorate, wrap or box your gift so it's fun to receive. Throughout *Gifts from the Kitchen*, there are ideas for dressing up everything from preserves to play dough, and candy to casseroles.

A tricky area when gifting something is whether you want the container returned or not. If you'd like the container back, put a piece of masking tape on the bottom. In pencil or indelible ink, write "Please return to:" and your name.

Always include the recipe. This helps to avoid allergic reactions, and if they enjoy the dish, they can make it again! Label items outside of the wrapping with any special instructions, such as cooking time, best-before date or chilling or storage techniques.

Finally, don't feel pressured to bring a gift to every occasion. But if the hostess of a party says you're not expected to bring anything, it's still acceptable to take a small loaf or a small bottle of wine, especially if you've made it yourself!

If you're stuck for ideas, the following is a list of events and appropriate gift suggestions:

Anniversary: Celebrate a wedding anniversary with a gift of baking, candy or dessert. Pull out all the stops with a bottle of homemade liqueur or a beverage mix, complete with two matching glasses. Or pick something fun from Gifts for the Home to spruce up the devoted couple's home—indoors or outdoors.

Baby Shower: Wrapping up a box of truffles to satisfy cravings or making a basket of assorted soothing bath products will make any new mom smile. Of course, desserts such as cakes and pies can be enjoyed by everyone at the shower or taken home by the mom-to-be to share with visiting relatives.

Birthday: Wrap a tray of appetizers with cellophane and a pretty bow to show it's a treat. How about a basket of muffins for the birthday boy or girl to grab as a snack for school or work? A sampling of candy would surely be dandy, or bundle up a few homemade condiments. Look in the Dry Mixes section for special coffee mixes, or in Liqueurs & Beverages for a wonderful concoction. Gifts for the Home section will provide great ideas for the birthday person's kitchen wall.

Corporate Gifts: Congratulate a promoted co-worker with a special cake from the Desserts section. Send a box of mints from the Candy section to show your appreciation for a job well done. Celebrate an anniversary with a bag of dry mix, such as cappuccino, along with two mugs or a bottle of spiced wine from Liqueurs & Beverages.

Illness or Death: When people are recovering from an illness, injury or a beloved one's death, meals are often haphazard. Come to the rescue with a thoughtful gift of food from the Dinners section. Choose a pan of lasagne, a pot roast or a casserole. Because these situations are not celebratory, presentation should be low-key. Keep it simple.

Moving: When someone you love moves far away, or even across town, why not make up a batch of specialty tea or coffee from the Dry Mixes section? Or put together a snack for the road—they'll think of you as they travel to their new home!

Welcome to the Neighborhood/Housewarming: Appetizers, whether they're to be eaten immediately or frozen for future entertaining, are great for people who've just moved into a new house or apartment. Or try a large bag of ready-to-make soup mix. Baked items are always welcome, as is candy, but how about giving a gift of condiments packaged with barbecue or picnic accessories? When most people move into a house, they're busy unpacking or doing renovations, so the gift of a dinner is always welcome!

Appetizers

Make a batch or two of these savory treats to take to a party, or put together a freezer plate for your favorite partygoer to use when he or she has company. Include decorative crackers with antipasto or a basket of fruit with a sweet dip and you'll get rave reviews.

As a fun change of pace, make a date with friends and family for an appetizer exchange. Everyone will enjoy the conversation and fellowship.

Crab Tarts, page 20

FROM THE KITCHEN OF

Strawberry Butter

A sweet spread with a soft pink color.
Deliver in a basket with a package of bagels.

Butter (or hard margarine), softened	1/2 cup	125 mL
Icing (confectioner's) sugar	1/2 cup	125 mL
Strawberry jam	1/4 cup	60 mL

Beat butter in medium bowl until light and fluffy. Add icing sugar. Beat. Add strawberry jam. Beat until light and fluffy. Place in airtight container. Chill. Makes 1 cup (250 mL).

2 tsp. (10 mL): 53 Calories; 3.9 g Total Fat; 47 mg Sodium; trace Protein; 5 g Carbohydrate; trace Dietary Fiber

Pictured on page 9.

DIRECTIONS FOR

Strawberry Butter: Keep chilled. Bring to room temperature just before serving. Serve with toast, buns, bagels or crackers.

Chocolate Peanut Spread

Great for kids of all ages to spread on warm toast.

Semisweet chocolate chips	1/2 cup	125 mL
Hard margarine (or butter)	2 tbsp.	30 mL
Smooth peanut butter	1 cup	250 mL

Heat and stir chocolate chips and margarine in small heavy saucepan on low until melted. Remove from heat.

Mix in peanut butter. Cool. Place in airtight container. Store in cupboard. Makes 1 1/2 cups (375 mL).

1 tbsp. (15 mL): 90 Calories; 7.6 g Total Fat; 62 mg Sodium; 3 g Protein; 4 g Carbohydrate; 1 g Dietary Fiber

Pictured on page 9.

Photo Legend previous page:

1. Piña Colada Dip, this page
2. Spinach Dip In A Loaf, page 11
3. Pink Fruit Dip, page 11
4. Cinnamon Spread, this page
5. Chocolate Peanut Spread, above
6. Strawberry Butter, above
7. Seafood Dip In A Loaf, page 11

Cinnamon Spread

This spread melts nicely on warm toast. Why not include a loaf of raisin bread and a pretty butter knife as part of your gift?

Hard margarine (or butter), softened	1/2 cup	125 mL
Brown sugar, packed	1/2 cup	125 mL
Ground cinnamon	1 tbsp.	15 mL

Mix all 3 ingredients well in small bowl. Place in airtight container. Store in cupboard. Makes 3/4 cup (175 mL).

1 tbsp. (15 mL): 105 Calories; 7.7 g Total Fat; 94 mg Sodium; trace Protein; 10 g Carbohydrate; trace Dietary Fiber

Pictured on page 9.

Piña Colada Dip

This creamy, pale yellow dip is excellent with fresh fruit.

Can of crushed pineapple, with juice	14 oz.	398 mL
Milk	3/4 cup	175 mL
Coconut milk	1/2 cup	125 mL
Cream cheese, softened and cut up	4 oz.	125 g
Package of instant vanilla pudding powder (4 serving size)	1	1

Measure pineapple with juice, milk and coconut milk into blender. Process until smooth.

Add cream cheese. Process until smooth. Add pudding powder. Process until well blended. Turn into serving bowl. Chill. Makes 3 2/3 cups (900 mL).

2 tbsp. (30 mL): 45 Calories; 2.4 g Total Fat; 64 mg Sodium; 1 g Protein; 6 g Carbohydrate; trace Dietary Fiber

Pictured on page 8.

Pink Fruit Dip

Put into a pretty container and add to a basket of fresh fruit. For a twist, this dip is also yummy with an assortment of cookies.

Light cream cheese (8 oz., 250 g, each), softened	2	2
Package of strawberry-flavored gelatin (jelly powder)	3 oz.	85 g
Jars of marshmallow crème (7 oz., 200 g, each)	2	2

Mash all 3 ingredients in medium bowl. Mix until smooth. Chill. Makes 2 cups (500 mL).

2 tbsp. (30 mL): 116 Calories; 5.3 g Total Fat; 206 mg Sodium; 3 g Protein; 15 g Carbohydrate; 0 g Dietary Fiber

Pictured on page 8.

Seafood Dip In A Loaf

Because of the shrimp, this dip should have a short time period between when it leaves your refrigerator and when it arrives at its destination.

Cream cheese, softened	8 oz.	250 g
Grated part-skim mozzarella cheese	1 cup	250 mL
Light sour cream	1/4 cup	60 mL
Light salad dressing (or mayonnaise)	1/4 cup	60 mL
Lemon juice	1 tsp.	5 mL
Seasoned salt	1 tsp.	5 mL
Chopped green onion	1/2 cup	125 mL
Seafood sauce	2 tbsp.	30 mL
Can of broken shrimp, drained and rinsed	4 oz.	113 g
Can of crabmeat, drained, cartilage removed, flaked	4 1/4 oz.	120 g
Round (or oblong) bread loaf	1	1

Beat first 8 ingredients together in medium bowl until smooth.

Mix in shrimp and crab. Chill. Makes 3 1/2 cups (875 mL) dip.

Cut top from loaf. Remove bread from inside loaf, leaving 1 inch (2.5 cm) thick shell. Cut removed bread into bite-size pieces. Place in plastic bag. Fill loaf with dip. Wrap in foil.

2 tbsp. (30 mL) dip only: 57 Calories; 4.6 g Total Fat; 141 mg Sodium; 3 g Protein; 1 g Carbohydrate; trace Dietary Fiber

Pictured on page 8.

Spinach Dip In A Loaf

This is one of the most popular dips for fresh veggies, bread cubes and crackers. Your gift will be well received—and enjoyed!

Package of frozen chopped spinach, thawed and squeezed dry	10 oz.	300 g
Sour cream	1 cup	250 mL
Salad dressing (or mayonnaise)	1 cup	250 mL
Chopped green onion	1/3 cup	75 mL
Envelope of dry vegetable soup mix (such as Knorr)	2 1/2 oz.	71 g
Grated Monterey Jack cheese	1 cup	250 mL
Round (or oblong) bread loaf	1	1

Combine first 6 ingredients in medium bowl. Chill. Makes 3 1/3 cups (825 mL) dip.

Cut top from loaf. Remove bread from inside loaf, leaving 1 inch (2.5 cm) thick shell. Cut removed bread into bite-size pieces. Place in plastic bag. Fill loaf with dip. Wrap in foil.

2 tbsp. (30 mL) dip only: 85 Calories; 7.1 g Total Fat; 261 mg Sodium; 2 g Protein; 4 g Carbohydrate; trace Dietary Fiber

Pictured on page 8 and page 9.

DIRECTIONS FOR

Seafood Dip or Spinach Dip In A Loaf: Place foil-wrapped loaf on baking sheet. Heat in 300 °F (150 °C) oven for about 2 hours. Place on large serving dish. Turn back foil. Surround with bread pieces.

How To

Bows

Have you ever wondered how to make a fancy bow to top off that special present? Here's how! And with the availability of wire-edged ribbon, it's even easier—you can even create "waves" in the tails.

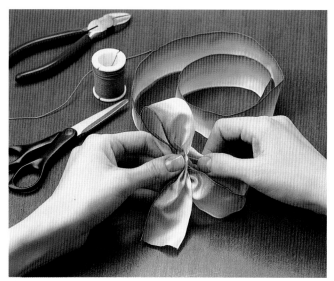

Materials: Ribbon, scissors, 26-gauge wire, wire cutters.

1. Cut a piece of ribbon approximately 39 inches (1 meter) long. Pinch between thumb and forefinger, about 3 inches (7.5 cm) from one end. Create a loop about 4 inches (10 cm) in diameter and pinch between thumb and forefinger.

2. Twisting ribbon at the pinch, make second loop for other side, finishing with a twist and pinch in the center. Make a third small loop for the center, finishing with a twist and pinch in the center.

3. Continue making loops of various sizes on either side, twisting and pinching for each loop, until there are three or more loops per side. Cut 8 inch (20 cm) piece of wire with wire cutters. Thread wire through smallest loop and wrap around twisted center portion.

4. Tie off wire in back of bow. Fluff out bow loops.

5. Fold ends of ribbon together and trim diagonally.

How To

Cellophane Wrapping

Rolls of cellophane, as well as excelsior, are available at most craft stores. This is a great way to give a "basketful of goodies."

Materials: Excelsior (or other packing material), basket, roll of cellophane (clear or patterned), scissors, raffia (or ribbon), tape.

1. Place enough excelsior in bottom of basket to allow items to be displayed in a pleasing way. Roll out a portion of the cellophane. Set basket on cellophane.

2. With long edge of basket parallel to edge of roll, pull up cellophane from under basket to desired height. Be sure to leave approximately 8 inches (20 cm) above handle to tie. Cut cellophane straight across.

3. Holding cellophane in center, gather in sides upwards just above handle, ensuring edges are straight. Sides should form triangles. Tie with raffia (or ribbon). Tighten cellophane by pulling upwards through tie.

4. Tuck excess cellophane underneath bottom of basket and tape.

Veggie Salsa

*This hot, slightly sweet salsa is a trendy gift.
If you accompany it with a bag of tortilla chips,
it will be an instant hit!*

Chopped jalapeño peppers (about 6 – 8), see Note	3/4 cup	175 mL
Coarsely chopped red onion	2 cups	500 mL
Coarsely chopped green pepper	1 1/2 cups	375 mL
Garlic cloves, minced	3 – 4	3 – 4
Can of tomato paste	5 1/2 oz.	156 mL
White vinegar	1/2 cup	125 mL
Coarsely chopped fresh parsley	1/2 cup	125 mL
Ground cumin	1/2 tsp.	2 mL
Cans of diced tomatoes (28 oz., 796 mL, each), with juice	2	2

Combine all 9 ingredients in large saucepan. Bring to a boil. Boil gently, uncovered, for about 45 minutes, stirring occasionally. Fill hot sterilized pint (2 cup, 500 mL) jars with salsa to within 3/4 inch (2 cm) of top. Place sterilized metal lids on jars and screw metal bands on securely. Process in a boiling water bath for 20 minutes. Makes 8 cups (2 L), enough for 8 half pint or 4 pint jars.

2 tbsp. (30 mL): 11 Calories; 0.1 g Total Fat; 42 mg Sodium; trace Protein; 3 g Carbohydrate; trace Dietary Fiber

Pictured on page 15.

Note: Wear thin rubber gloves when cutting hot peppers (such as jalapeño, habanero and Thai) to avoid the caustic oily compound (capsaicin) that gives the peppers their heat. Avoid touching your eyes.

Antipasto

Do all the chopping first—and there's a lot! Some people use their food processor but you may prefer the results when done by hand. It takes longer, but the chunkier texture is worth it.

Small cauliflower	1	1
Can of ripe pitted olives, drained and finely chopped	14 oz.	398 mL
Jar of pimiento-stuffed olives, drained and finely chopped	26 oz.	750 mL
Jar of pickled onions, drained and finely chopped	13 oz.	375 mL
Cooking oil	1 cup	250 mL
Can of sliced mushrooms, drained and coarsely chopped	10 oz.	284 mL
Jars of pimiento (2 oz., 57 mL, each), drained and finely chopped	2	2
Sweet mixed pickles, drained and finely chopped	4 cups	1 L
Can of cut green beans, drained and finely chopped	14 oz.	398 mL
Medium green pepper, finely chopped	1	1
Ketchup	3 1/2 cups	875 mL
Chili sauce (or ketchup)	2 cups	500 mL
White vinegar	1/2 cup	125 mL
Can of baby (or broken) shrimp, drained, rinsed and coarsely chopped	4 oz.	113 g
Cans of flaked tuna (6 oz., 170 g, each), drained	2	2

Combine first 5 ingredients in large uncovered pot or Dutch oven. Bring to a boil. Boil for 10 minutes, stirring often.

Add next 8 ingredients. Bring to a boil. Boil for 10 minutes, stirring often.

Mix in shrimp and tuna. Fill freezer containers to within 1 inch (2.5 cm) of top. Seal tightly. Freeze. Makes about 18 cups (4.5 L).

2 tbsp. (30 mL): 85 Calories; 2.9 g Total Fat; 350 mg Sodium; 9 g Protein; 6 g Carbohydrate; 1 g Dietary Fiber

Pictured on page 15 and page 153.

DIRECTIONS FOR

Antipasto: Can be stored covered in refrigerator for up to one week after thawing. Serve with crackers.

Left: Antipasto, above
Right: Veggie Salsa, this page

Shrimp Ball

The perfect hostess gift for somebody who
does a lot of entertaining over the holidays.

Cream cheese, softened	8 oz.	250 g
Salad dressing (or mayonnaise)	2 tbsp.	30 mL
Hard margarine (or butter), softened	1/4 cup	60 mL
Grated Havarti cheese	1 1/2 cups	375 mL
Minced onion	1–2 tbsp.	15–30 mL
Ground rosemary	1/2 tsp.	2 mL
Dried sweet basil	1 tsp.	5 mL
Garlic powder	1/8 tsp.	0.5 mL
Lemon juice	1 1/2 tbsp.	25 mL
Cans of broken shrimp (4 oz., 113 g, each), drained and rinsed	2	2
Parsley flakes	1 1/2 tbsp.	25 mL
Paprika	1 tsp.	5 mL

Beat cream cheese, salad dressing and margarine together in medium bowl until smooth.

Add next 6 ingredients. Mix well.

Add shrimp. Mix well. Chill. Form into a ball.

Sprinkle parsley and paprika on sheet of waxed paper. Roll cheese ball in parsley mixture until well coated. Makes 3 cups (750 mL).

2 tbsp. (30 mL): 96 Calories; 8.4 g Total Fat; 126 mg Sodium; 4 g Protein; 1 g Carbohydrate; trace Dietary Fiber

Pictured on page 17.

DIRECTIONS FOR

Shrimp Ball: Keep chilled until ready to serve. Arrange on plate surrounded by assorted crackers.

Brie En Croûte

Give with a box of crackers or a few apples
and you'll be a favorite guest.

Box of frozen puff pastry patty shells, thawed (6 per box)	1	1
Brie cheese rounds (4 oz., 125 g, each)	3	3
Egg yolk (large)	1	1
Water	1 tbsp.	15 mL

Roll 2 shells out on lightly floured surface to 6 inch (15 cm) circle.

Place Brie cheese in middle of 1 pastry. Top with remaining pastry. Dampen edges with water. Crimp and seal edges together. Set on ungreased baking sheet. Repeat with remaining patty shells and cheese.

Fork-beat egg yolk and water together in small cup. Brush tops of pastry. Bake in 375°F (190°C) oven for about 20 minutes until golden. Makes 3 rounds. Each round cuts into 8 wedges, for a total of 24 wedges.

1 wedge: 124 Calories; 9.4 g Total Fat; 130 mg Sodium; 4 g Protein; 6 g Carbohydrate; 0 g Dietary Fiber

Pictured on page 17.

DIRECTIONS FOR

Brie En Croûte: Arrange on ungreased baking sheet. Heat in 375°F (190°C) oven for about 10 minutes. Let stand for 10 minutes before cutting into wedges. Serve with crackers or fruit.

Cheese Roll

This cheese log has a Christmas look to it with the paprika and
green pepper. Freezes well and makes a great hostess gift.

Grated light sharp Cheddar cheese	2 cups	500 mL
Cream cheese, softened	8 oz.	250 g
Finely chopped green pepper	1 tbsp.	15 mL
Finely chopped red pepper	1 tbsp.	15 mL
Sliced hazelnuts (filberts), toasted	1/2 cup	125 mL
Garlic powder	1/4 tsp.	1 mL
Seasoned salt	1/4 tsp.	1 mL
Paprika, approximately	1 tbsp.	15 mL

Combine first 7 ingredients in medium bowl. Mix well. Form into roll about 1 1/2 inches (3.8 cm) in diameter and about 10 inches (25 cm) long.

Sprinkle paprika on sheet of waxed paper. Roll cheese roll in paprika until completely coated. Wrap in plastic wrap. Chill. Makes 1 roll. Cuts into about 40 slices.

1 slice: 42 Calories; 3.6 g Total Fat; 63 mg Sodium; 2 g Protein; 1 g Carbohydrate; trace Dietary Fiber

Pictured on page 17.

DIRECTIONS FOR

Cheese Roll: Keep chilled. Let stand at room temperature for 15 minutes before cutting into thin slices.

Top Left and Centre: Brie En Croûte, this page
Top Right (Green Cellophane): Shrimp Ball, this page
Bottom Left: Cheese Roll, above

Ham Turnovers

The secret to keeping pastry edges together is to dampen
them before sealing. For a more decorative look,
use a fancy-edged cookie cutter. Tasty.

Cans of ham flakes (6 1/2 oz., 184 g, each), drained	2	2
Can of condensed cream of mushroom soup	10 oz.	284 mL
Onion flakes, crushed	2 tsp.	10 mL
Sweet pickle relish	1 tbsp.	15 mL
Jar of chopped pimiento, drained	2 oz.	57 mL
Dry bread crumbs	1/3 cup	75 mL
Pastry, enough for 4 single crusts, your own or a mix		
Large egg, fork-beaten	1	1

Combine ham, soup, onion flakes, relish, pimiento and bread crumbs in medium bowl. Stir well. Makes 3 3/4 cups (925 mL) filling.

Roll out pastry on lightly floured surface to 1/8 inch (3 mm) thickness. Cut into 3 inch (7.5 cm) circles. Place 1 1/2 tsp. (7 mL) filling just off center of each circle. Dampen edges all around. Fold over. Pinch seams to seal. Cut small slit in tops. Place on greased baking sheet.

Brush tops with egg. Bake in 400°F (205°C) oven for about 40 minutes until lightly browned. Makes 64 turnovers.

1 turnover: 74 Calories; 4.6 g Total Fat; 165 mg Sodium; 2 g Protein; 6 g Carbohydrate; trace Dietary Fiber

Pictured on page 19.

DIRECTIONS FOR
Ham Turnovers: Arrange on ungreased baking sheet. Heat in 325°F (160°C) oven for about 10 minutes.

Pizza Shortbread

These look like refrigerator cookies but are more like crackers.
Mellow, buttery flavor with a hint of an Italian taste.

All-purpose flour	2 cups	500 mL
Hard margarine (or butter), softened	1 cup	250 mL
Grated Parmesan cheese	1/2 cup	125 mL
Finely chopped pimiento	2 tbsp.	30 mL
Dried whole oregano	1 tsp.	5 mL
Dried sweet basil	1/4 tsp.	1 mL
Paprika, sprinkle (optional)		

Combine first 6 ingredients in medium bowl. Mix until dough can be kneaded into a ball. Shape into 2 rolls about 1 1/2 inches (3.8 cm) in diameter. Cut into 1/4 inch (6 mm) slices. Arrange on ungreased baking sheet.

Sprinkle each slice with paprika. Bake in 375°F (190°C) oven for about 10 minutes until golden. Makes 46 shortbread appetizers.

1 appetizer: 64 Calories; 4.6 g Total Fat; 71 mg Sodium; 1 g Protein; 5 g Carbohydrate; trace Dietary Fiber

Pictured on page 19.

Spinach & Cheese Mini-Quiches

Because the frozen tart shells are already in foil cups,
these delectable cheese morsels are ready for gift-giving.
Wonderful blend of flavors.

Grated sharp Cheddar cheese	1 cup	250 mL
Frozen chopped spinach, thawed and squeezed dry	10 oz.	300 g
Frozen mini-tart shells, thawed	24	24
Large egg, fork-beaten	1	1
Milk	1/2 cup	125 mL
Parsley flakes	1/2 tsp.	2 mL
Salt	1/4 tsp.	1 mL
Pepper	1/8 tsp.	0.5 mL
Onion powder	1/8 tsp.	0.5 mL

Divide cheese and spinach among tart shells. Place on ungreased baking sheet.

Combine remaining 6 ingredients in small bowl. Spoon 1 tbsp. (15 mL) egg mixture into each shell. Bake in 350°F (175°C) oven for 20 to 25 minutes. Makes 24 mini-quiches.

1 mini-quiche: 60 Calories; 4 g Total Fat; 109 mg Sodium; 2 g Protein; 4 g Carbohydrate; trace Dietary Fiber

Pictured on page 19.

DIRECTIONS FOR
Spinach And Cheese Mini-Quiches: Arrange on ungreased baking sheet. Heat in 325°C (160°C) oven for about 10 minutes.

Top Left: Ham Turnovers, page 18
Bottom Left: Surprise Cheese Puffs, below

Top Right: Spinach And Cheese Mini-Quiches, page 18
Bottom Right: Pizza Shortbread, page 18

Surprise Cheese Puffs

*These are wonderful pop-in-your-mouth appetizers.
Keep chilled so they don't flatten in your gift container.
The surprise is a pickle in the middle.*

Hard margarine (or butter), softened	1/2 cup	125 mL
Grated sharp Cheddar cheese	2 cups	500 mL
Salt	1/2 tsp.	2 mL
Paprika	1 tsp.	5 mL
Cayenne pepper	1/8 tsp.	0.5 mL
All-purpose flour	1 cup	250 mL
Gherkin pieces (size of green stuffed olives)	84	84

Cream first 5 ingredients together in medium bowl.

Add flour. Mix well.

Mold 1 tsp. (5 mL) dough around 1 gherkin piece until covered completely. Repeat with remaining dough and gherkins. Arrange on ungreased baking sheet. Chill until firm. Bake in 400°F (205°C) oven for about 15 minutes. Makes about 84 appetizers.

1 appetizer: 35 Calories; 2.1 g Total Fat; 103 mg Sodium; 1 g Protein; 3 g Carbohydrate; trace Dietary Fiber

Pictured above.

*DIRECTIONS FOR
Surprise Cheese Puffs: To serve warm, arrange on ungreased baking sheet. Heat in 325°F (160°C) oven for about 10 minutes. Can also be served at room temperature.*

Crab Tarts, below

Crunchies, below

Crab Tarts

For a quick gift, use prepared tart shells instead of making your own.
Very nice flavor to these.

PASTRY

Hard margarine (or butter), softened	1/2 cup	125 mL
Cream cheese, softened	8 oz.	250 g
All-purpose flour	1 1/2 cups	375 mL
Dill weed	1 tsp.	5 mL

FILLING

Large eggs	5	5
Half-and-half cream	1/2 cup	125 mL
Grated Havarti (or Swiss) cheese	1 1/4 cups	300 mL
Can of crabmeat, drained, cartilage removed, flaked	4 1/4 oz.	120 g
Minced onion flakes	1 tsp.	5 mL
Parsley flakes	1 tsp.	5 mL
Worcestershire sauce	1/4 tsp.	1 mL
Salt	1/4 tsp.	1 mL
Pepper	1/8 tsp.	0.5 mL

Paprika (optional)

Pastry: Cream margarine and cream cheese together in medium bowl. Add flour and dill weed. Mix well. Form into a ball. Chill for 1 hour.

Filling: Beat eggs in large bowl until frothy

Add next 8 ingredients. Mix well. Set aside. Roll out pastry on lightly floured surface. Cut into circles to fit into ungreased muffin cups. Spoon filling into shells, about 3/4 full.

Sprinkle with paprika. Bake in 400°F (205°C) oven for about 15 minutes until golden and set.Makes about 60 tarts.

1 tart: 60 Calories; 4.4 g Total Fat; 67 mg Sodium; 2 g Protein;
3 g Carbohydrate; trace Dietary Fiber

Pictured above and on page 7.

DIRECTIONS FOR
Crab Tarts: Arrange on ungreased baking sheet. Heat in 325°F
(160°C) oven for about 10 minutes.

Crunchies

These delightful little morsels have the texture of shortbread
mixed with the crunchiness of a crisp rice cereal.

All-purpose flour	1 1/2 cups	375 mL
Grated sharp Cheddar cheese	1 1/2 cups	375 mL
Hard margarine (or butter), softened	2/3 cup	150 mL
Baking powder	1 tsp.	5 mL
Salt	1/2 tsp.	2 mL
Cayenne pepper	1/4 tsp.	1 mL
Crisp rice cereal (such as Rice Crispies)	1 cup	250 mL

Combine first 6 ingredients in medium bowl. Mix well.

Add cereal. Mix with hands. Shape into 1 inch (2.5 cm) balls. Arrange on ungreased baking sheet. Bake in 375°F (190°C) oven for 20 minutes until lightly browned. Makes 3 1/2 dozen appetizers.

1 appetizer: 64 Calories; 4.5 g Total Fat; 107 mg Sodium; 2 g Protein;
4 g Carbohydrate; trace Dietary Fiber

Pictured above.

Baking

Does anything say "thoughtful" better
than homemade baking? Even as you
mix up the batter, you're thinking of
how much the person receiving your gift will enjoy sampling
your latest creation with a cup of tea or a mug of coffee.

Maybe you know a cookie lover who would love to receive a batch
of tasty morsels fresh from your oven or a sweet tooth whose eyes
will light up at the sight of a pan of squares. And for those rare
moments of peace and quiet, who wouldn't welcome the chance to
cuddle up with a good book and a scrumptious piece of coffee cake?

Orange Pinwheels, page 24

Breads & Buns

Does your mouth water in anticipation when you smell fresh bread and buns baking? Count on the same reaction from family and friends when you appear at their doorstep bearing a basket of freshly made goodies.

There is nothing like the warm goodness of a loaf of bread, whether on its own or with a bowl of soup. A gift of sweet buns offered in congratulations for a promotion or a loaf of cheesy bread presented as a thank-you is certain to be gladly received.

Here's your chance to pass along a little goodness to someone special.

Photo Legend previous page:

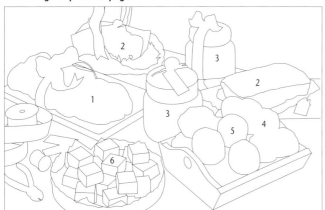

Orange Pinwheels

Give this gift right in the new pan it was baked in! Include instructions to serve slightly warmed so that the sauce is nice and gooey when the buns are turned out of the pan.

SYRUP		
Prepared orange juice	1/2 cup	125 mL
Granulated sugar	1/4 cup	60 mL
Brown sugar, packed	1/4 cup	60 mL
Hard margarine (or butter)	1 tbsp.	15 mL
Grated orange peel, packed	1 tsp.	5 mL
BISCUITS		
All-purpose flour	2 cups	500 mL
Baking powder	1 tsp.	5 mL
Salt	1/2 tsp.	2 mL
Hard margarine (or butter)	6 tbsp.	100 mL
Milk	7/8 cup	200 mL
Brown sugar, packed	2 tbsp.	30 mL
Ground cinnamon	1/2 tsp.	2 mL

Syrup: Combine all 5 ingredients in small saucepan. Heat and stir until margarine is melted. Pour into greased 9 x 9 inch (22 x 22 cm) pan.

Biscuits: Put first 3 ingredients into large bowl. Cut in margarine until crumbly. Make a well in center.

Pour milk into well. Stir until just moistened and mixture forms a ball of dough. Turn out onto lightly floured surface. Knead 6 times. Roll out into 9 x 16 inch (22 x 40 cm) rectangle.

Combine brown sugar and cinnamon in small cup. Sprinkle over dough. Roll up, jelly-roll style, beginning at long end. Cut into sixteen 1 inch (2.5 cm) thick slices. Place, cut side down, on top of syrup. Bake in 425°F (220°C) oven for 25 minutes until lightly browned. Makes 16 pinwheels.

1 pinwheel: 149 Calories; 5.4 g Total Fat; 166 mg Sodium; 2 g Protein; 23 g Carbohydrate; 1 g Dietary Fiber

Pictured on front cover and on page 21.

DIRECTIONS FOR
Orange Pinwheels: Heat buns in pan in 300°F (150°C) oven for about 15 minutes to warm slightly. Invert onto serving plate.

Challa

KHAH-lah is sometimes made in a four-strand braid, but you may find three strands easier. This is a showpiece loaf, large enough to make a perfect centerpiece. You can also divide the dough and make two smaller braids.

Warm water	1/2 cup	125 mL
Granulated sugar	1 tsp.	5 mL
Envelope of active dry yeast (or 2 1/2 tsp., 12 mL, bulk)	1/4 oz.	8 g
Very warm (not hot) water	1/2 cup	125 mL
Hard margarine (or butter), melted	3 tbsp.	50 mL
Granulated sugar	2 tbsp.	30 mL
Salt	2 tsp.	10 mL
Large eggs	3	3
All-purpose flour	2 cups	500 mL
All-purpose flour	3 cups	750 mL
TOPPING		
Large egg, fork-beaten	1	1
Water	1 tbsp.	15 mL

Stir first amounts of water and sugar in small bowl until sugar is dissolved. Sprinkle yeast over top. Let stand for 10 minutes. Stir to dissolve yeast.

Combine second amount of water and margarine in large bowl. Cool until lukewarm. Beat in second amount of sugar, salt and eggs. Add yeast mixture. Beat until smooth.

Add first amount of flour. Beat on low until smooth. Work in second amount flour until dough pulls away from sides of bowl. Turn out onto lightly floured surface. Knead for 5 to 10 minutes until smooth and elastic. Place dough in greased bowl, turning once to grease top. Cover with tea towel. Let stand in oven with light on and door closed for about 1 1/4 hours until doubled in bulk. Punch dough down. Divide dough into 3 equal portions. Roll each portion into 26 inch (65 cm) rope. Lay ropes side by side down length of greased baking sheet. Pinch 3 ends together. Braid ropes. Pinch remaining 3 ends together. Tuck ends under. Cover with tea towel. Let stand in oven with light on and door closed for about 35 minutes until almost doubled in size.

Topping: Combine egg and water in small bowl. Brush dough with egg mixture. Bake in 400°F (205°C) oven for 20 to 25 minutes until golden. Makes 1 large braid. Cuts into 24 slices.

1 slice: 133 Calories; 2.6 g Total Fat; 229 mg Sodium; 4 g Protein; 23 g Carbohydrate; 1 g Dietary Fiber

Pictured on page 22.

Panettone

Originating in Italy, the pan-uh-TOH-nee is traditionally served at Christmas, however, it is appropriate for any type of celebration.

Warm water	1/2 cup	125 mL
Granulated sugar	2 tsp.	10 mL
Envelopes of active dry yeast, 1/4 oz., 8 g, each (or 5 tsp., 25 mL, bulk)	2	2
Large eggs, fork-beaten	4	4
Very warm milk	3/4 cup	175 mL
Hard margarine (or butter), melted	1/2 cup	125 mL
Granulated sugar	1/4 cup	60 mL
Brown sugar, packed	1/3 cup	75 mL
Salt	1 1/2 tsp.	7 mL
Grated lemon peel	2 tbsp.	30 mL
Aniseed (or flavoring), lightly crushed	1 tsp.	5 mL
All-purpose flour, approximately	6 1/2 cups	1.6 L
Golden raisins	1 cup	250 mL
Chopped mixed glazed fruit	1 cup	250 mL
Chopped glazed cherries	1/3 cup	75 mL
Hard margarine (or butter), softened	1 tsp.	5 mL

Stir water and sugar in small bowl until sugar is dissolved. Sprinkle yeast over top. Let stand for 10 minutes. Stir to dissolve yeast.

Combine next 8 ingredients in large bowl. Add yeast mixture. Beat until smooth.

Mix in enough flour until dough pulls away from sides of bowl. Turn out onto lightly floured surface. Knead for about 5 minutes until smooth and elastic. Place in greased bowl, turning once to grease top. Cover with tea towel. Let stand in oven with light on and door closed for about 1 1/2 hours until doubled in bulk. Punch dough down. Roll or press dough into large square or rectangle.

Sprinkle raisins, fruit and cherries over top. Roll up, jelly-roll style. Cut into 2 equal portions. Place 1 portion in each of 2 greased 9 x 5 x 3 inch (22 x 12.5 x 7.5 cm) loaf pans. Cover with tea towel. Let stand in oven with light on and door closed for about 1 hour until doubled in size. Bake in 350°F (175°C) oven for about 30 minutes. Place on wire rack to cool.

Brush warm tops with margarine. Makes 2 loaves. Each loaf cuts into 12 slices, for a total of 24 slices.

1 slice: 264 Calories; 5.6 g Total Fat; 222 mg Sodium; 6 g Protein; 48 g Carbohydrate; 2 g Dietary Fiber

Pictured on page 29.

How To

Crackle Painting

Crackle painting takes a bit of time since each coat must dry, but the weathered faux antique look is worth the effort.

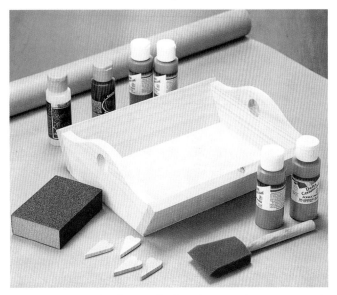

Materials: Wooden box, roll of craft paper (or newspaper), sanding sponge (or sandpaper), damp cloth, paint brush, dark latex base paint, clear crackle paint medium, light latex top coat paint, wood cut-outs, contrasting paint, glue gun.

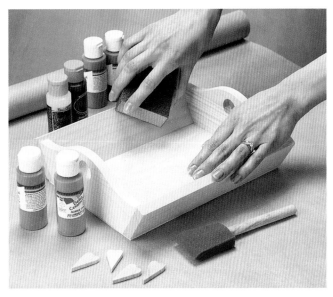

1. Place wooden box on craft paper to protect table or counter. Sand item to even out irregular surface and create texture for paint to adhere to. Wipe off dust with damp cloth.

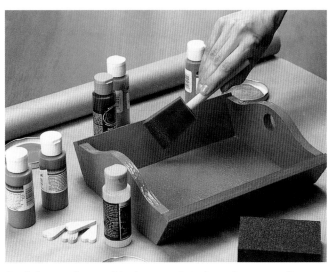

2. Paint surface with base paint. Let dry according to manufacturer's instructions. Paint surface with clear crackle paint medium. Let dry according to manufacturer's instructions.

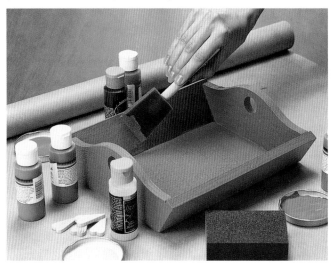

3. Paint surface with top coat paint. Let dry according to manufacturer's instructions.

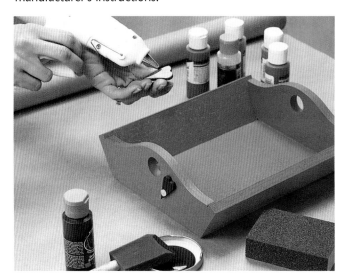

4. Paint cut-outs with contrasting color of paint. Affix with glue gun.

Fabric Loaf Wrap

Using fabric, a tea towel or other linen to wrap a food gift means you not only have an eye-catching dressing, but also a handy re-usable item to offer. This quick and easy method requires few tools.

Materials: Loaf wrapped in plastic wrap, 20 x 22 inch (50 x 55 cm) piece of fabric, scissors.

1. Place loaf, top side up, diagonally on fabric. Fold one corner over long side of loaf and tuck underneath.

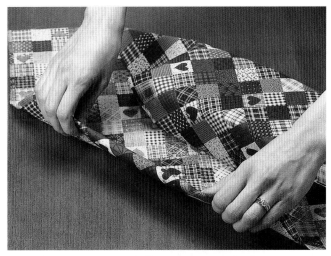

2. Fold opposite corner halfway in to meet loaf.

3. Fold onto top of loaf, creating a smooth edge.

4. Gathering fabric at one end of loaf, fold up to middle. Without letting go of that end, repeat with other side. Tie in a knot. Fluff out tails of knot and trim any loose threads.

Bubble Baubles

These baubles are fun embellishments on cellophane-wrapped gifts.

Materials: Iridescent cellophane, scissors, 1 inch (2.5 cm) Styrofoam balls, fishing line, 18 inch (45 cm) pieces of 26-gauge wire, wire cutters, pencil (or pen).

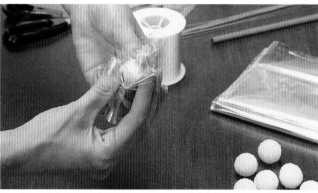

1. Cut 4 inch (10 cm) squares of iridescent cellophane. Wrap one square around each Styrofoam ball, gathering up edges and twisting firmly.

2. Tie twist of each ball with fishing line, close to base. Trim fishing line and wrap ends tightly.

3. Wrap the 18 inch (45 cm) lengths of wire in coil around pencil. Wrap each wire in different tightnesses and lengths. Poke end of wire into Styrofoam ball near tail stub, through iridescent cellophane. Arrange on gift in desired lengths.

Savory Bubble Bread

Perfect for sharing with friends because the pieces (or "bubbles") pull off easily—no slicing required.

Frozen loaf of bread dough, thawed	1	1
Hard margarine (or butter), melted	3 tbsp.	50 mL
Dill weed	1 tsp.	5 mL
Dried rosemary	1 tsp.	5 mL
Celery salt	1/4 tsp.	1 mL
Garlic powder	1/2 tsp.	2 mL
Grated Parmesan cheese	3/4 cup	175 mL

Cut dough into 20 portions. Shape into balls.

Combine next 5 ingredients in small saucepan. Dip balls, 1 at a time, into mixture.

Put Parmesan cheese on plate. Roll each ball in cheese. Arrange in greased 8 x 4 x 3 inch (20 x 10 x 7.5 cm) loaf pan. Cover with tea towel. Let stand in oven with light on and door closed for about 45 minutes until doubled in size. Bake in 375°F (190°C) oven for about 25 minutes until golden. Let stand in pan for 10 to 15 minutes. Turn out onto wire rack to cool. Makes 1 loaf. Pulls into 20 pieces.

1 piece: 95 Calories; 3.8 g Total Fat; 232 mg Sodium; 4 g Protein; 12 g Carbohydrate; 1 g Dietary Fiber

Pictured on page 29.

Jiffy Cheese Biscuits

Crispy outside with a light fluffy texture inside.

All-purpose flour	2 cups	500 mL
Baking powder	4 tsp.	20 mL
Granulated sugar	4 tsp.	20 mL
Salt	1/2 tsp.	2 mL
Hard margarine (or butter)	1/2 cup	125 mL
Grated sharp Cheddar cheese	2 cups	500 mL
Water	1 1/3 cups	325 mL

Combine flour, baking powder, sugar and salt in large bowl. Cut in margarine until crumbly.

Add cheese and water. Mix. Drop by tablespoonfuls onto greased baking sheet. Bake in 400°F (205°C) oven for 20 minutes until lightly browned. Makes 24 biscuits.

1 biscuit: 119 Calories; 7.4 g Total Fat; 220 mg Sodium; 4 g Protein; 9 g Carbohydrate; trace Dietary Fiber

Pictured on page 29.

Top Left: Jiffy Cheese Biscuits, above
Top Right: Savory Bubble Bread, above
Center and Bottom: Panettone, page 25

Savory Bread

A dense loaf with a distinctive onion flavor.
Wrap with a new wooden breadboard.

Warm water	1/2 cup	125 mL
Granulated sugar	1 tsp.	5 mL
Envelope of active dry yeast	1/4 oz.	8 g
(or 2 1/2 tsp., 12 mL, bulk)		
Warm water	2 cups	500 mL
Cooking oil	1/4 cup	60 mL
Envelope of dry onion soup mix	1 1/4 oz.	38 g
Salt	2 tsp.	10 mL
Granulated sugar	1/4 cup	60 mL
Grated Parmesan cheese	1/3 cup	75 mL
All-purpose flour, approximately	6 1/4 cups	1.5 L
Hard margarine (or butter), softened	2 tsp.	10 mL

Muffin Buns, this page   Savory Bread, this page

Stir first amount of water and sugar in small bowl until sugar is dissolved. Sprinkle yeast over top. Let stand for 10 minutes. Stir to dissolve yeast.

Combine next 6 ingredients in large bowl. Add yeast mixture. Beat until smooth.

Gradually add flour until dough pulls away from sides of bowl. Turn out onto lightly floured surface. Knead for about 10 minutes until smooth and elastic. Place in greased bowl, turning once to grease top. Cover with tea towel. Let stand in oven with light on and door closed for about 1 1/2 hours until doubled in bulk. Punch dough down. Cut into 2 portions. Shape into loaves. Place 1 portion in each of 2 greased 9 x 5 x 3 inch (22 x 12.5 x 7.5 cm) loaf pans. Cover with tea towel. Let stand in oven with light on and door closed for 45 to 50 minutes until doubled in size. Bake in 375°F (190°C) oven for 20 to 25 minutes. Turn out onto wire rack to cool.

Brush warm tops with margarine. Makes 2 loaves. Each loaf cuts into 12 slices, for a total of 24 slices.

1 slice: 171 Calories; 3.6 g Total Fat; 371 mg Sodium; 4 g Protein; 30 g Carbohydrate; 1 g Dietary Fiber

Pictured on this page.

Muffin Buns

An honest-to-goodness homemade white dinner bun.

Warm water	1/4 cup	60 mL
Granulated sugar	1 tsp.	5 mL
Envelope of active dry yeast	1/4 oz.	8 g
(or 2 1/2 tsp., 12 mL, bulk)		

Very warm (not hot) milk	1 cup	250 mL
Cooking oil	2 tbsp.	30 mL
Granulated sugar	2 tbsp.	30 mL
Large egg, fork-beaten	1	1
Salt	1 tsp.	5 mL
All-purpose flour	3 1/2 cups	875 mL
Hard margarine (or butter), softened	1 tsp.	5 mL

Stir water and first amount of sugar in small bowl until sugar is dissolved. Sprinkle yeast over top. Let stand for 10 minutes. Stir to dissolve yeast.

Combine next 5 ingredients in large bowl. Add yeast mixture. Beat until smooth.

Add flour, in 3 or 4 additions, mixing well after each addition. Turn out onto lightly floured surface. Knead until smooth. Place in greased bowl, turning once to grease top. Cover with tea towel. Let stand in oven with light on and door closed for about 1 hour until doubled in bulk. Punch dough down. Form into 12 buns. Place in greased muffin cups. Cover with tea towel. Let stand in oven with light on and door closed for about 35 minutes until doubled in size. Bake on bottom rack in 400°F (205°C) oven for about 15 minutes. Turn out onto wire rack to cool.

Brush warm tops with margarine. Makes 12 buns.

1 bun: 190 Calories; 3.7 g Total Fat; 219 mg Sodium; 5 g Protein; 33 g Carbohydrate; 1 g Dietary Fiber

Pictured above.

Soft Pretzels

Having these to munch on while watching a major sporting event will fast become a tradition with your friends. No rising required.

Warm water	1/2 cup	125 mL
Granulated sugar	1 tsp.	5 mL
Envelope of active dry yeast (2 1/2 tsp., 12 mL, bulk)	1/4 oz.	8 g
Warm water	1 cup	250 mL
Granulated sugar	1 tbsp.	15 mL
Salt	1/2 tsp.	2 mL
All-purpose flour, approximately	3 3/4 cups	925 mL
Large egg, fork-beaten	1	1
Water	1 tbsp.	15 mL

Coarse salt, sprinkle
Sesame seeds, sprinkle

Stir first amount of water and sugar in small bowl until sugar is dissolved. Sprinkle yeast over top. Let stand for 10 minutes. Stir to dissolve yeast.

Stir second amounts of water and sugar in large bowl until sugar is dissolved. Add salt and yeast mixture.

Gradually mix in flour until stiff dough forms. Turn out onto lightly floured surface. Knead for about 5 minutes until smooth and elastic. Let rest for 10 minutes. Divide dough into 12 equal portions. Roll each portion into 15 inch (37.5 cm) rope. Shape each rope into pretzel. Arrange on greased baking sheets.

Combine egg with remaining water. Brush tops of each pretzel.

Sprinkle salt and sesame seeds over pretzels. Bake in 425°F (220°C) oven for about 15 minutes. Makes 12 pretzels.

1 pretzel: 164 Calories; 0.9 g Total Fat; 105 mg Sodium; 5 g Protein; 33 g Carbohydrate; 1 g Dietary Fiber

Pictured on this page.

Cookies & Squares

Nothing brings back memories of childhood like dunking cookies in milk, so pass the tradition along to a child in your life. For the adults, offer them a square, the perfectly grown-up treat to have with coffee. Go a little wild with something unique like a cookie pizza and children of all ages will know you're tempting them with the very best. Fill up a decorative jar or tin for friends and be sure to include the recipe so that when it comes time for a refill they can make the recipe themselves!

Crowd-Pleasing Cookie Pizza

The taste of a cookie with the look of a pizza.
What a fun gift to give.

CRUST		
Hard margarine (or butter), softened	1/2 cup	125 mL
Brown sugar, packed	3/4 cup	175 mL
Large egg	1	1
Vanilla	1 tsp.	5 mL
All-purpose flour	1 1/2 cups	375 mL
TOPPING		
Milk chocolate chips	1 cup	250 mL
Miniature marshmallows	1 cup	250 mL
Finely chopped pecans (optional)	1/2 cup	125 mL
Can of sweetened condensed milk	11 oz.	300 mL
Candy-coated chocolate candies (such as M & M's)	1/2 cup	125 mL

Crust: Cream margarine and brown sugar together in large bowl until light and fluffy. Beat in egg and vanilla until well blended.

Add flour. Stir. Turn out onto lightly floured surface. Knead until soft dough forms. Press dough into 12 inch (30 cm) greased pizza pan, forming rim around edge.

Topping: Sprinkle chocolate chips, marshmallows and pecans evenly over crust. Pour condensed milk evenly over top. Bake in 350°F (175°C) oven for 20 minutes until crust is golden.

Immediately place candies on top. Cool completely in pan. Cuts into about 16 wedges.

1 wedge: 321 Calories; 13.4 g Total Fat; 127 mg Sodium; 5 g Protein; 47 g Carbohydrate; 1 g Dietary Fiber

Pictured on page 33.

1. Crowd-Pleasing Cookie Pizza, above
2. Colored Swirls, page 35
3. Chip Choc Banana Cookies, page 34
4. Two-Layer Brownies, page 35
5. Pineapple Brownies, page 36
6. Mocha Brownies, page 35

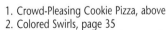

Chip Choc Banana Cookies

*A cake-like cookie that would go great
as a gift with specialty coffees.*

Hard margarine (or butter), softened	1 cup	250 mL
Brown sugar, packed	1 cup	250 mL
Large eggs	2	2
Vanilla	1 tsp.	5 mL
Mashed banana	1 cup	250 mL
All-purpose flour	2 1/2 cups	625 mL
Cocoa	1/2 cup	125 mL
Baking powder	2 tsp.	10 mL
Baking soda	1/2 tsp.	2 mL
Ground cinnamon	2 tsp.	10 mL
Milk chocolate chips	1 1/2 cups	375 mL

Cream margarine and brown sugar together in large bowl until light and fluffy. Beat in eggs and vanilla until well blended. Add banana. Beat until well mixed.

Combine flour, cocoa, baking powder, baking soda and cinnamon in medium bowl. Gradually add to banana mixture until well blended.

Add chocolate chips. Stir until evenly distributed. Drop by level tablespoonfuls onto greased cookie sheet. Bake in 350°F (175°C) oven for about 14 minutes. Makes about 60 cookies.

*1 cookie: 94 Calories; 4.9 g Total Fat; 68 mg Sodium; 1 g Protein;
12 g Carbohydrate; 1 g Dietary Fiber*

Pictured on page 33.

TIP

To make squares easier to remove and cut, line pan with foil. If you are cutting them immediately, pull the foil away from the edges. Otheriwse, bring the foil up over the edges and simply add another piece of foil over top. Rewrap entirely in one more layer, ready to give as a gift or freeze for later use.

Double Chocolate Cookies

*These are crisp on the outside and soft on the inside.
Dark and white chunks of chocolate peek through,
as well as bits of oatmeal and nuts. A very attractive
cookie to package for gift-giving.*

Hard margarine (or butter), softened	1 cup	250 mL
Brown sugar, packed	1 1/2 cups	375 mL
Large eggs	2	2
Vanilla	3/4 tsp.	4 mL
Plain yogurt	1/2 cup	125 mL
All-purpose flour	2 1/2 cups	625 mL
Quick-cooking rolled oats (not instant)	2 1/2 cups	625 mL
Baking powder	1/2 tsp.	2 mL
Baking soda	1 tsp.	5 mL
Salt	1/2 tsp.	2 mL
Semisweet chocolate baking squares (1 oz., 28 g, each), chopped	4	4
White chocolate baking squares (1 oz., 28 g, each), chopped	4	4
Walnuts (or pecans), chopped (optional)	1 cup	250 mL

Cream margarine and brown sugar together in large bowl until light and fluffy. Beat in eggs and vanilla until well blended. Add yogurt. Beat until well mixed.

Combine flour, rolled oats, baking powder, baking soda and salt in medium bowl. Gradually add to margarine mixture until well blended.

Stir in both chocolates and walnuts. Drop by tablespoonfuls onto greased cookie sheet. Flatten with floured fork or bottom of glass. Bake in 350°F (175°C) oven for 12 to 15 minutes. Makes about 60 cookies.

*1 cookie: 69 Calories; 3.1 g Total Fat; 56 mg Sodium; 1 g Protein;
10 g Carbohydrate; trace Dietary Fiber*

Pictured on page 23.

Colored Swirls

A very pretty cookie that's not too sweet.

Hard margarine (or butter), softened	1 cup	250 mL
Granulated sugar	1 cup	250 mL
Large egg	1	1
Half-and-half cream	2 tbsp.	30 mL
Almond flavoring	1 tsp.	5 mL
All-purpose flour	3 cups	750 mL
Baking soda	1/2 tsp.	2 mL
Salt	1/4 tsp.	1 mL
Semisweet chocolate baking square, melted	1 oz.	28 g
Maraschino cherries, well drained and chopped	1/3 cup	75 mL
Drops of red food coloring	5	5
Finely chopped pistachio nuts	1/2 cup	125 mL
Drops of green food coloring	10	10

Cream margarine and sugar together in large bowl until light and fluffy.

Beat in egg, cream and almond flavoring until well blended.

Combine flour, baking soda and salt in medium bowl. Gradually add to margarine mixture until well blended. Divide dough into 3 portions. Place each portion in separate bowls.

Add chocolate to 1 portion of dough. Mix well. Add cherries and red food coloring to another portion. Mix well. Add pistachio nuts and green food coloring to remaining portion. Mix well. Roll out each portion separately on waxed paper to 14 x 9 inch (35 x 22 cm) rectangle, about 1/8 inch (3 mm) thick. Place chocolate layer on red layer. Top with green layer. Trim to make edges even. Roll up, jelly-roll style, starting with long side. Wrap in plastic wrap. Chill overnight. Remove plastic wrap. Let stand for 10 minutes. Slice about 1/4 inch (6 mm) thick with warm knife. Place on lightly greased cookie sheet. Bake in 375°F (190°C) oven for about 10 minutes until lightly browned. Cool for 10 minutes. Transfer to wire rack to cool completely. Makes about 36 cookies.

1 cookie: 133 Calories; 7 g Total Fat; 114 mg Sodium; 2 g Protein; 16 g Carbohydrate; 1 g Dietary Fiber

Pictured on page 33.

Two-Layer Brownies

A rich fudgey brownie layer with a cream cheese layer on top. Only for those who like to receive decadent desserts. Heavenly!

Packages of brownie mix (15 1/2 oz., 440 g, each)	2	2
Cooking oil	1/2 cup	125 mL
Large eggs	4	4
All-purpose flour	1/4 cup	60 mL
Light cream cheese, softened	8 oz.	250 g
Icing (confectioner's) sugar	3 cups	750 mL
Large eggs	2	2

Combine first 4 ingredients in medium bowl. Mix well. Turn into greased 9 x 13 inch (22 x 33 cm) pan.

Beat cream cheese and icing sugar together in medium bowl until smooth. Beat in second amount of eggs, 1 at a time, beating well after each addition. Pour over brownie mixture. Bake in 350°F (175°C) oven for about 35 minutes until firm and lightly browned. Cuts into 30 brownies.

1 brownie: 138 Calories; 6 g Total Fat; 89 mg Sodium; 2 g Protein; 20 g Carbohydrate; trace Dietary Fiber

Pictured on page 33.

Mocha Brownies

A quick and easy coffee-flavored brownie.

Can of sweetened condensed milk	11 oz.	300 mL
Semisweet chocolate chips	1 cup	250 mL
Vanilla	1 tsp.	5 mL
Instant coffee granules	1 1/2 tbsp.	25 mL
Salt	1/4 tsp.	1 mL
Graham cracker crumbs	2 cups	500 mL
Chopped walnuts (optional)	1/2 cup	125 mL

Combine first 5 ingredients in medium bowl. Mix well.

Add graham crumbs and walnuts. Mix well. Turn into greased 8 x 8 inch (20 x 20 cm) pan. Bake in 350°F (175°C) oven for about 25 minutes. Cuts into 25 brownies.

1 brownie: 115 Calories; 4.2 g Total Fat; 87 mg Sodium; 2 g Protein; 18 g Carbohydrate; 1 g Dietary Fiber

Pictured on page 33.

Pineapple Brownies

*A tasty, moist brownie that is sure to please
all the chocolate lovers in your life.*

Hard margarine (or butter), softened	1/2 cup	125 mL
Granulated sugar	1 cup	250 mL
Large eggs	2	2
Vanilla	1 tsp.	5 mL
Can of crushed pineapple, well drained	8 oz.	227 mL
Cocoa	1/3 cup	75 mL
All-purpose flour	1 cup	250 mL
Salt	1/2 tsp.	2 mL
Chopped walnuts	1/2 cup	125 mL

Cream margarine and sugar together in medium bowl. Beat in eggs, 1 at a time. Add vanilla. Mix.

Add pineapple. Mix.

Add cocoa, flour, salt and walnuts. Mix. Turn into greased 9 x 9 inch (22 x 22 cm) pan. Bake in 350°F (175°C) oven for about 25 minutes. Wooden pick inserted in center should come out moist but without batter clinging to it. Cuts into 36 brownies.

1 brownie: 82 Calories; 4.2 g Total Fat; 68 mg Sodium; 1 g Protein; 10 g Carbohydrate; 1 g Dietary Fiber

Pictured on page 33.

Rainbow Squares, below

Rainbow Squares

A fruity burst of sweetness in a colorful pallette of pastels. These will disappear quickly if there are kids around.

Hard margarine (or butter)	1/4 cup	60 mL
Large marshmallows	32	32
Colored fruit loops-type cereal	6 cups	1.5 L

Combine margarine and marshmallows in large saucepan. Heat and stir until melted and smooth.

Place cereal in large bowl. Add marshmallow mixture. Toss to coat. Press into greased 9 x 9 inch (22 x 22 cm) pan, using dampened hands if too sticky. Let stand for 3 hours until firm. Cuts into 36 squares.

1 square: 55 Calories; 1.7 g Total Fat; 35 mg Sodium; trace Protein; 10 g Carbohydrate; trace Dietary Fiber

Pictured above.

Chewy Slice, below

Cracker Crunch, below

Chewy Slice

A pleasant nut-and-coconut square that's not too sweet.

FIRST LAYER

All-purpose flour	1 1/2 cups	375 mL
Brown sugar, packed	1/2 cup	125 mL
Hard margarine (or butter), softened	1/3 cup	75 mL

SECOND LAYER

Large eggs	2	2
Brown sugar, packed	1 cup	250 mL
Vanilla	1 tsp.	5 mL
Salt	1/4 tsp.	1 mL
Crisp rice cereal (such as Rice Krispies)	1 cup	250 mL
Chopped walnuts	1 cup	250 mL
Medium unsweetened coconut	1 cup	250 mL

First Layer: Combine flour and brown sugar in medium bowl. Cut in margarine until crumbly. Press into ungreased 9 x 9 inch (22 x 22 cm) pan. Bake in 350°F (175°C) oven for 15 minutes.

Second Layer: Beat eggs in large bowl until frothy. Add brown sugar, vanilla and salt. Beat until smooth.

Add remaining 3 ingredients to egg mixture. Mix. Spoon onto first layer. Bake for 25 minutes. Cool. Cuts into 36 squares.

1 square: 120 Calories; 5.9 g Total Fat; 54 mg Sodium; 2 g Protein; 15 g Carbohydrate; 1 g Dietary Fiber

Pictured above.

Cracker Crunch

An old favorite updated with cinnamon and chocolate chips. So yummy.

Whole graham crackers	30	30
Butter (not margarine)	1 cup	250 mL
Brown sugar, packed	1 cup	250 mL
Finely sliced (or chopped) almonds (or walnuts or pecans)	1 cup	250 mL
Ground cinnamon, light sprinkle (optional)		
Semisweet chocolate chips	3/4 cup	175 mL

Line greased 10 x 15 inch (25 x 38 cm) jelly roll pan with graham crackers, trimmed to fit edges.

Combine butter and brown sugar in medium saucepan. Heat and stir until starting to boil and sugar is dissolved. Boil for 3 minutes, without stirring. Pour evenly over graham crackers.

Sprinkle with almonds and cinnamon. Bake in 350°F (175°C) oven for 7 to 9 minutes until bubbly and edges are slightly browned.

Sprinkle with chocolate chips. Cool. Cuts into 30 pieces.

1 piece: 166 Calories; 11.1 g Total Fat; 115 mg Sodium; 2 g Protein; 16 g Carbohydrate; 1 g Dietary Fiber

Pictured above.

Nanaimo Bars

This traditional treat is probably one of the most well-received gifts from the kitchen. To be certain the bottom layer doesn't crumble when cut, mix the ingredients very well and pack firmly.

BOTTOM LAYER

Hard margarine (or butter)	3/4 cup	175 mL
Granulated sugar	1/4 cup	60 mL
Cocoa	6 tbsp.	100 mL
Large egg	1	1
Milk	1 tbsp.	15 mL
Vanilla	1 tsp.	5 mL
Graham cracker crumbs	2 cups	500 mL
Medium coconut	1 cup	250 mL
Chopped walnuts	1/2 cup	125 mL

SECOND LAYER

Hard margarine (or butter), softened	1/4 cup	60 mL
Milk	3 tbsp.	50 mL
Custard powder (or vanilla pudding powder)	2 tbsp.	30 mL
Icing (confectioner's) sugar	2 cups	500 mL

ICING

Semisweet chocolate baking squares (1 oz., 28 g, each), cut up	4	4
Hard margarine (or butter)	1 tbsp.	15 mL

Bottom Layer: Combine first 6 ingredients in large saucepan. Heat and stir until mixture resembles custard. Remove from heat.

Add graham crumbs, coconut and walnuts. Stir. Pack firmly in ungreased 9 x 9 inch (22 x 22 cm) pan. Chill.

Second Layer: Beat all 4 ingredients together in medium bowl until smooth. Spread over first layer. Chill.

Icing: Melt chocolate and margarine in medium saucepan on low, stirring often. Spread over second layer. Chill. Bring to room temperature before cutting to avoid cracking hard top layer. A hot dry knife helps. Cuts into 36 squares.

1 square: 174 Calories; 10.2 g Total Fat; 107 mg Sodium; 2 g Protein; 17 g Carbohydrate; 1 g Dietary Fiber

Pictured on page 22.

Chocolate Caramel Squares, below

Chocolate Caramel Squares

Sweet and crunchy with a nutty flavor. Somebody is going to know they're loved.

BOTTOM LAYER

All-purpose flour	1 cup	250 mL
Granulated sugar	1/4 cup	60 mL
Brown sugar, packed	1/4 cup	60 mL
Hard margarine (or butter), softened	1/2 cup	125 mL

FILLING

Semisweet chocolate chips	1/2 cup	125 mL
Milk chocolate chips	1/2 cup	125 mL
Caramel sauce	1/3 cup	75 mL

TOPPING

All-purpose flour	2/3 cup	150 mL
Brown sugar, packed	1/3 cup	75 mL
Hard margarine (or butter), softened	1/3 cup	75 mL
Finely chopped pecans	1/2 cup	125 mL

Bottom Layer: Combine first 3 ingredients in medium bowl. Cut in margarine until crumbly. Press firmly in greased 9 x 9 inch (22 x 22 cm) pan. Bake in 350°F (175°C) oven for 15 minutes.

Filling: Sprinkle bottom layer with both chocolate chips.

Drizzle caramel sauce over top chocolate chips.

Topping: Stir flour and brown sugar in medium bowl. Cut in margarine until crumbly. Add pecans. Stir. Sprinkle over caramel sauce. Bake in 350°F (175°C) oven for about 20 minutes until browned. Cuts into 36 squares.

1 square: 120 Calories; 7.2 g Total Fat; 60 mg Sodium; 1 g Protein; 14 g Carbohydrate; 1 g Dietary Fiber

Pictured above.

Nutty Biscotti

For the coffee lover on your list. In fact, even milk lovers will find these irresistible because who doesn't love to dunk?

Hard margarine (or butter), softened	1/4 cup	60 mL
Large eggs	2	2
Egg white (large)	1	1
Granulated sugar	3/4 cup	175 mL
Vanilla	1 tsp.	5 mL
Frangelico liqueur (optional)	1 tbsp.	15 mL
All-purpose flour	2 1/2 cups	625 mL
Baking soda	1 tsp.	5 mL
Salt	1/4 tsp.	1 mL
Flaked hazelnuts (filberts), toasted (see Note)	2/3 cup	150 mL

Cream first 6 ingredients together in large bowl until smooth.

Add flour, baking soda, salt and hazelnuts. Mix well. Turn out onto lightly floured surface. Knead 6 times. Place on greased baking sheet. Shape into 16 inch (40 cm) long log, 1 1/4 inches (3 cm) in diameter. Bake in 350°F (175°C) oven for 30 minutes. Cool on wire rack for 10 to 15 minutes. Reduce oven temperature to 275°F (140°C). Cut rolls diagonally into 1/2 inch (12 mm) slices. Arrange on same baking sheet. Bake for 10 to 12 minutes. Turn slices over. Turn off oven. Let stand in oven for 30 minutes until crisp. Makes 24 biscotti.

1 biscotti: 123 Calories; 4.7 g Total Fat; 110 mg Sodium; 3 g Protein; 18 g Carbohydrate; 1 g Dietary Fiber

Pictured on front cover and on page 129.

Note: To toast nuts or seeds, place in single layer in ungreased shallow pan. Bake in 350°F (175°C) oven for 5 to 10 minutes, stirring or shaking often, until desired doneness.

Variation: Melt 3/4 cup (175 mL) semisweet chocolate chips in small saucepan on low, stirring often. Dip ends of biscotti into chocolate. Place on waxed paper. Chill until firm.

Choco Cran Biscotti

The sweet taste of chocolate with bursts of tart cranberry! Package the whole recipe or give a few slices with a mug or container of specialty ground coffee.

Dried cranberries	1 cup	250 mL
Prepared orange juice	3 tbsp.	50 mL
Hard margarine (or butter), softened	1/4 cup	60 mL
Granulated sugar	1/2 cup	125 mL
Large eggs	3	3
All-purpose flour	2 cups	500 mL
Cocoa	1/3 cup	75 mL
Baking powder	1 tsp.	5 mL
Salt	1/4 tsp.	1 mL

Combine cranberries and orange juice in microwave-safe dish. Cover. Microwave on high (100%) for 1 minute. If cranberries are not soft, heat for 30 second intervals until softened.

Cream margarine, sugar and eggs together in large bowl until smooth. Add cranberry mixture. Stir.

Add flour, cocoa, baking powder and salt. Mix well. Turn out onto lightly floured surface. Knead 6 times. Place on greased baking sheet. Shape into 16 inch (40 cm) long log, 1 1/4 inches (3 cm) in diameter. Bake in 350°F (175°C) oven for 30 minutes. Cool on wire rack for 10 to 15 minutes. Reduce oven temperature to 275°F (140°C). Cut rolls diagonally into 1/2 inch (12 mm) slices. Arrange on same baking sheet. Bake for 10 to 12 minutes. Turn slices over. Turn off oven. Let stand in oven for 30 minutes until crisp. Makes 24 biscotti.

1 biscotti: 203 Calories; 3.4 g Total Fat; 74 mg Sodium; 10 g Protein; 34 g Carbohydrate; 1 g Dietary Fiber

Pictured on front cover.

TIP

Biscotti, an Italian biscuit-cookie that has been baked twice, freezes very well or can be stored at room temperature in an airtight container.

Muffins, Loaves & Coffee Cakes

Delicious fruit and streusel toppings beckon in these baked concoctions, a sure hit at any office, shower or potluck party. You'll find an impressive variety of recipes for muffins, loaves and coffee cakes, perfect for any occasion.

Dress up a basket of muffins or a loaf of bread with some of the decorating tips and ideas shown throughout this section. The person you're offering it to will feel special knowing you went that extra mile.

Pumpkin Streusel Muffins

The nice light texture of these muffins is hidden beneath a nutty streusel topping. Spicy, nutty and a wee bit sweet.

All-purpose flour	2 cups	500 mL
Granulated sugar	1/2 cup	125 mL
Baking powder	1 tbsp.	15 mL
Ground cinnamon	1/2 tsp.	2 mL
Ground nutmeg	1/4 tsp.	1 mL
Ground ginger	1/4 tsp.	1 mL
Ground cloves	1/8 tsp.	0.5 mL
Salt	1/2 tsp.	2 mL
Large egg, fork-beaten	1	1
Cooking oil	1/3 cup	75 mL
Canned pumpkin (no spices)	1 cup	250 mL
Milk	2/3 cup	150 mL
STREUSEL TOPPING		
Hard margarine (or butter)	1 tbsp.	15 mL
Brown sugar, packed	1/4 cup	60 mL
Ground cinnamon	1/2 tsp.	2 mL
Finely chopped walnuts (or pecans)	1/4 cup	60 mL

Combine first 8 ingredients in large bowl. Make a well in center.

Beat egg, cooking oil, pumpkin and milk together in medium bowl. Add to well. Stir until just moistened. Fill 12 greased muffin cups about 3/4 full.

Streusel Topping: Melt margarine in small saucepan. Stir in brown sugar, cinnamon and walnuts. Divide and sprinkle over each muffin. Bake in 400°F (205°C) oven for about 18 minutes. Wooden pick inserted in center of muffin should come out clean. Let stand in pan for 5 minutes before removing muffins to wire rack to cool. Makes 12 muffins.

1 muffin: 235 Calories; 9.8 g Total Fat; 219 mg Sodium; 4 g Protein; 34 g Carbohydrate; 1 g Dietary Fiber

Pictured on page 23.

Zucchini Nut Muffins, below

Cranberry Muffins

Slightly sweet, slightly tangy and just the right balance between the two. The bright red cranberry pieces make this such a pretty and delicious gift.

Chopped fresh (or frozen, thawed) cranberries	1 cup	250 mL
Granulated sugar	1/3 cup	75 mL
Large egg	1	1
Granulated sugar	1/3 cup	75 mL
Cooking oil	1/4 cup	60 mL
Milk	1 cup	250 mL
All-purpose flour	2 cups	500 mL
Baking powder	1 tbsp.	15 mL
Salt	1/2 tsp.	2 mL

Combine cranberries and first amount of sugar in small bowl. Set aside.

Beat egg, second amount of sugar and cooking oil together in large bowl. Add milk. Mix.

Combine flour, baking powder and salt in medium bowl. Add to egg mixture. Stir until just moistened. Add cranberry mixture. Stir gently. Fill 12 greased muffin cups 3/4 full. Bake in 400°F (205°C) oven for 18 to 20 minutes. Wooden pick inserted in center of muffin should come out clean. Let stand in pan for 5 minutes before removing muffins to wire rack to cool. Makes 12 muffins.

1 muffin: 242 Calories; 5.9 g Total Fat; 209 mg Sodium; 7 g Protein; 40 g Carbohydrate; 1 g Dietary Fiber

Pictured on page 23.

Zucchini Nut Muffins

A breakfast muffin that's not too sweet. They're a great way to use up some of the zucchini that grows in your garden.

All-purpose flour	2 cups	500 mL
Granulated sugar	1/2 cup	125 mL
Baking powder	2 tsp.	10 mL
Baking soda	1/2 tsp.	2 mL
Salt	1/2 tsp.	2 mL
Ground cinnamon	3/4 tsp.	4 mL
Ground ginger	1/8 tsp.	0.5 mL
Large egg, fork-beaten	1	1
Cooking oil	1/3 cup	75 mL
Grated zucchini, with peel	1 cup	250 mL
Milk	1/2 cup	125 mL
Almond flavoring	1/4 tsp.	1 mL
Vanilla	1/4 tsp.	1 mL
Chopped pecans (or walnuts)	1/2 cup	125 mL

Combine first 7 ingredients in large bowl. Make a well in center.

Add remaining 7 ingredients to well. Stir until just moistened. Fill 12 greased muffin cups 3/4 full. Bake in 400°F (205°C) oven for 18 minutes. Wooden pick inserted in center should come out clean. Let stand in pan for 5 minutes before removing muffins to wire rack to cool. Makes 12 muffins.

1 muffin: 218 Calories; 10.6 g Total Fat; 226 mg Sodium; 4 g Protein; 28 g Carbohydrate; 1 g Dietary Fiber

Pictured above.

Apricot Loaf

Paula

Fruit Loaf

Pineapple Banana Mini-Loaves

Yummy! Banana bread with a pineapple twist.

All-bran cereal	1 cup	250 mL
Can of crushed pineapple, with juice	8 oz.	227 mL
Hard margarine (or butter), melted	1/2 cup	125 mL
Granulated sugar	2/3 cup	150 mL
Large eggs	2	2
Mashed banana (about 3 medium)	1 cup	250 mL
Vanilla	1 tsp.	5 mL
Chopped walnuts (optional)	1/2 cup	125 mL
All-purpose flour	1 1/2 cups	375 mL
Baking powder	2 tsp.	10 mL
Baking soda	1/2 tsp.	2 mL
Salt	1/2 tsp.	2 mL

Combine cereal and pineapple with juice in small bowl. Let stand for 10 minutes, stirring 2 or 3 times.

Beat margarine and sugar in large bowl until smooth. Beat in eggs, 1 at a time. Add pineapple mixture, banana and vanilla. Mix. Stir in walnuts.

Combine flour, baking powder, baking soda and salt in medium bowl. Add to banana mixture. Stir until just moistened. Turn into nine greased 4 x 2 1/4 x 1 1/4 inch (10 x 5.75 x 3.5 cm) mini-loaf pans. Bake in 350°F (175°C) oven for 30 minutes. Wooden pick inserted in center should come out clean. Let stand in pans for 5 minutes before removing loaves to wire rack to cool. Makes 9 mini-loaves.

1 mini-loaf: 315 Calories; 12.4 g Total Fat; 497 mg Sodium; 5 g Protein; 49 g Carbohydrate; 4 g Dietary Fiber

Pictured on page 43.

Photo Legend previous page:

1. Strawberry Mini-Loaves, page 45
2. Apricot Loaf, page 45
3. Pineapple Banana Mini-Loaves, above
4. Fruit Loaf, this page

Variation: Turn into greased 9 x 5 x 3 inch (22 x 12.5 x 7.5 cm) loaf pan. Bake in 350°F (175°C) oven for 65 minutes. Wooden pick inserted in center should come out clean. Let stand in pan for 15 minutes before removing loaf to wire rack to cool. Makes 1 loaf. Cuts into 18 slices.

Fruit Loaf

A smaller loaf, but every slice is full of nuts, fruit and peel. Cuts better on the second day.

Hard margarine (or butter), softened	1/4 cup	60 mL
Granulated sugar	2/3 cup	150 mL
Large egg	1	1
Vanilla	1/2 tsp.	2 mL
Chopped pecans (or walnuts)	1/2 cup	125 mL
Chopped cranberries	1/3 cup	75 mL
Chopped glazed orange peel	1/3 cup	75 mL
Golden raisins, coarsely chopped	1/3 cup	75 mL
Milk	3/4 cup	175 mL
All-purpose flour	2 cups	500 mL
Baking powder	2 tsp.	10 mL
Salt	1/2 tsp.	2 mL

Cream margarine, sugar, egg and vanilla together in large bowl until smooth.

Add pecans, cranberries, orange peel, raisins and milk. Stir.

Combine flour, baking powder and salt in medium bowl. Add to fruit mixture. Stir until just moistened. Turn into greased 8 x 4 x 3 inch (20 x 10 x 7.5 cm) loaf pan. Bake in 350°F (175°C) oven for 60 minutes. Wooden pick inserted in center should come out clean. Let stand in pan for 15 minutes before removing loaf to wire rack to cool. Makes 1 loaf. Cuts into 14 slices.

1 slice: 206 Calories; 7.2 g Total Fat; 191 mg Sodium; 3 g Protein; 33 g Carbohydrate; 1 g Dietary Fiber

Pictured on page 42.

TIP

To prevent baked gifts from becoming soggy, allow breads, buns and pretzels to cool completely before wrapping.

Strawberry Mini-Loaves

Wonderful strawberry flavor! Bits of strawberry throughout.

Hard margarine (or butter), softened	1/4 cup	60 mL
Granulated sugar	2/3 cup	150 mL
Large egg	1	1
Vanilla	1/2 tsp.	2 mL
Sliced fresh (or frozen) strawberries	2 cups	500 mL
Lemon juice	1 tsp.	5 mL
All-purpose flour	2 cups	500 mL
Baking powder	2 tsp.	10 mL
Baking soda	1 tsp.	5 mL
Salt	1/2 tsp.	2 mL

Cream margarine and sugar together in large bowl. Beat in egg and vanilla.

Cut up strawberries. Mash, a few at a time, adding berries with any juice to egg mixture. Add lemon juice. Stir.

Combine flour, baking powder, baking soda and salt in medium bowl. Add to strawberry mixture. Stir until just moistened. Turn into greased mini-bundt pans. Bake in 350°F (175°C) oven for about 30 minutes. Wooden pick inserted in center should come out clean. Let stand in pans for 10 minutes before removing loaves to wire rack to cool. Makes 6 mini-bundt loaves.

1 mini-bundt loaf: 353 Calories; 9.6 g Total Fat; 643 mg Sodium; 6 g Protein; 61 g Carbohydrate; 3 g Dietary Fiber

Pictured on page 43.

Variation: Turn batter into greased 9 x 5 x 3 inch (22 x 12.5 x 7.5 cm) loaf pan. Bake in 350°F (175°C) oven for about 1 hour. Wooden pick inserted in center should come out clean. Let stand in pan for 15 minutes. Turn out onto wire rack to cool. Makes 1 loaf. Cuts into 18 slices.

Apricot Loaf

Let stand overnight for best flavor.

Hard margarine (or butter), softened	1/2 cup	125 mL
Granulated sugar	2/3 cup	150 mL
Large egg	1	1
Vanilla	1 tsp.	5 mL
Milk	3/4 cup	175 mL
All-purpose flour	2 1/4 cups	550 mL
Baking powder	1 1/2 tsp.	7 mL
Salt	3/4 tsp.	4 mL
Chopped dried apricots (see Note)	1 cup	250 mL

Cream margarine and sugar together in large bowl. Beat in egg. Add vanilla and milk. Mix.

Combine flour, baking powder, salt and apricots in medium bowl. Add to egg mixture. Stir until just moistened. Turn into greased 9 x 5 x 3 inch (22 x 12.5 x 7.5 cm) loaf pan. Bake in 350°F (175°C) oven for about 60 minutes. Wooden pick inserted in center should come out clean. Let stand in pan for 15 minutes before removing to wire rack to cool. Makes 1 loaf. Cuts into 18 slices.

1 slice: 166 Calories; 6 g Total Fat; 203 mg Sodium; 3 g Protein; 26 g Carbohydrate; 1 g Dietary Fiber

Note: If dried apricots are excessively dry, pour boiling water over them in small bowl. Soak for 10 to 15 minutes. Drain. Dry on paper towel. Chop.

APRICOT MINI-LOAVES: Turn batter into 6 clay pots, 4 inches (10 cm) in diameter across top, that have been soaked in water for 15 minutes. Bake in 350°F (175°C) oven for about 30 minutes. Wooden pick inserted in center should come out clean. Let stand in pots for 10 minutes. Turn out onto to wire racks to cool. Makes 6 mini-loaves.

Pictured on page 42/43.

Easiest Cinnamon Treats

Take these sweet and cinnamony treats hot out of the oven to a deserving neighbor.

Chopped pecans (or walnuts)	3 tbsp.	50 mL
Hard margarine (or butter)	1/4 cup	60 mL
Brown sugar, packed	2/3 cup	150 mL
Vanilla	1/2 tsp.	2 mL
Ground cinnamon	3/4 tsp.	4 mL
Package of refrigerator country-style biscuits (10 biscuits per tube)	1	1

Sprinkle pecans in bottom of greased 9 inch (22 cm) round cake pan.

Melt margarine in small saucepan. Add brown sugar, vanilla and cinnamon. Stir. Set aside.

Arrange biscuits over pecans. Spoon margarine mixture over top, being sure to cover every biscuit. Bake, uncovered, in 400°F (205°C) oven for 15 minutes until biscuits are risen and browned. Invert onto serving plate. Makes 10 biscuits.

1 biscuit: 213 Calories; 10.4 g Total Fat; 395 mg Sodium; 2 g Protein; 29 g Carbohydrate; trace Dietary Fiber

Pictured on page 51.

How To

Clay Pot Cooking

Goodies baked in clay pots are unique in their presentation and visually appealing, plus they can have a crisper crust than those baked in conventional metal bakeware.

Clay cookware provides even heat distribution and heat retention, making it a wonderful option for baking breads, loaves and casseroles. There are two distinct types of clay cookware: earthenware (low-fired) and stoneware (high-fired). Both can be purchased glazed or unglazed. They are appropriate for use in the oven but cannot be used on top of the stove.

Earthenware is fired at temperatures between 1940°F and 2100°F (1060°C and 1150°C). If unglazed, it is very porous and must be completely immersed in water for about 15 minutes just before using. (New earthenware should be soaked for 30 minutes and then scrubbed with a brush to remove any fine dust before being used the first time.) The damp vessel, filled with the recipe, is then placed in a cold oven and heated slowly as the oven warms up. If you are converting recipes that use conventional bakeware, a general guideline is to add 100°F (32°C) to the temperature and 30 minutes to the cooking time.

Earthenware plant pots, found at department stores and greenhouses, can be used for baking bread and loaves. Presoaking is recommended, but you could instead line it with foil.

Don't place clay pots in the dishwasher. Instead, let the vessel cool, then soak it in water with a few tablespoons of baking soda or a few drops of detergent. Since the clay is porous, strong detergents are not recommended because they will be absorbed. Scrubbing with salt and a brush is another good cleaning alternative. If there is a lid it should be stored alongside, not on top of, the bottom section so that any excess water can evaporate. If strong flavors like garlic are to be cooked in a clay pot, line it first with foil or parchment paper to prevent the taste from transferring to the next recipe cooked in it.

Stoneware is made of clay that has been cured at temperatures up to 2300°F (1270°C). This type of cookware is safe for the oven, microwave and freezer and is generally used for commercial dinnerware and bakeware sets. If the dish (and food inside) has been chilled or frozen, it should be thawed to room temperature before placing in a hot oven.

Stoneware is not porous so it doesn't require seasoning or soaking in water before use, but food should be evenly distributed across its surface for best cooking results. The inside can be greased or lined with foil for easy cleanup, but neither is required.

Be sure to read the manufacturer's instructions on all clay cookware before starting.

How To

Embellishments

Looking for a way to dress up a jar of preserves? Need a little "doodad" for a pan of baking? If you don't want to rely on bows or wrapping paper, use embellishments to make gift special.

Craft stores, dollar stores and toy stores are full of ideas for embellishments. Also, check kitchenware stores for small accessories that tie in with the idea of what you're giving.

Look for plastic jalapeño peppers and a pair of pickle tongs to dress up a jar of Hot Pickled Peppers (shown on front cover).

Often the recipe you are making, or the reason you are considering it as a gift, will provide inspiration for the embellishment. Use ingredients such as cinnamon sticks for Easiest Cinnamon Treats (shown on page 51) or Spicy Sachet (shown on back cover). With a bit of patience, a portion of the recipe and a glue gun, you can make a fun lid for Cracker Snack Mix (shown on page 143).

Use plastic oranges to add zing to a bow tied around the Orange Pinwheels (shown on front cover) or a fun plastic pineapple on Pineapple Brownies (shown on page 33). Even liquors and liqueurs can get in on the act, with grapes and cinnamon sticks for Spiced Wine and strawberries for Strawberry Wine (both shown on page 137).

For the "foodies" on your list, include a pizza cutter with the Crowd-Pleasing Cookie Pizza (shown on page 33). Or tie some fun sundae spoons onto a gift of ice-cream sauces (shown on page 99). Embellishments can even be small toys, like plastic spiders, rats or skeletons when you're giving a Halloween gift (shown on page 61). Check out your local hardware store to make a nifty decoration for Nuts And Bolts (shown on page 142).

Pumpkin Loaf

This recipe will also make nine mini-loaves or three large stoneware pots—ideal for gift-giving. You'll enjoy this unique and tasty combination of pumpkin and orange.

Hard margarine (or butter), softened	1/4 cup	60 mL
Granulated sugar	1 cup	250 mL
Large eggs	2	2
Canned pumpkin (no spices)	1 cup	250 mL
Milk	1/2 cup	125 mL
All-purpose flour	2 cups	500 mL
Baking powder	2 tsp.	10 mL
Baking soda	1/2 tsp.	2 mL
Ground cinnamon	1 tsp.	5 mL
Ground nutmeg	1/2 tsp.	2 mL
Grated orange peel	2 tbsp.	30 mL
Salt	1 tsp.	5 mL
Chopped walnuts (or pecans), optional	1/2 cup	125 mL

Cream margarine and sugar together in large bowl. Beat in eggs, 1 at a time. Add pumpkin and milk. Mix.

Combine remaining 8 ingredients in medium bowl. Add to batter. Stir until just moistened. Turn into greased 9 x 5 x 3 inch (20 x 10 x 7.5 cm) loaf pan. Bake in 350°F (175°C) oven for about 50 minutes. Let stand in pan for 10 minutes. Turn out onto wire rack to cool. Makes 1 loaf. Cuts into 18 slices.

1 slice: 141 Calories; 3.5 g Total Fat; 252 mg Sodium; 3 g Protein; 25 g Carbohydrate; 1 g Dietary Fiber

Pictured on back cover.

Chocolate Spice Loaf

This old-fashioned spice loaf is full of nuts and raisins. The chocolate flavor is subtle but gives the loaf a darker coloring. For a unique wrapping, wrap the cooled loaf in plastic wrap and then check out Fabric Loaf Wrap on page 27, for a cloth carrying case.

Hard margarine (or butter), softened	1/2 cup	125 mL
Granulated sugar	1 cup	250 mL
Large eggs	2	2
Applesauce	1 cup	250 mL
Semisweet chocolate chips, melted	1/2 cup	125 mL
All-purpose flour	2 cups	500 mL
Baking powder	1 tsp.	5 mL
Baking soda	1/2 tsp.	2 mL
Salt	1/2 tsp.	2 mL
Ground cinnamon	1/2 tsp.	2 mL
Ground nutmeg	1/4 tsp.	1 mL
Ground allspice	1/8 tsp.	0.5 mL
Chopped walnuts	1/2 cup	125 mL
Raisins	3/4 cup	175 mL

Cream margarine and sugar together in large bowl. Beat in eggs, 1 at a time. Add applesauce. Stir. Mix in melted chocolate.

Combine remaining 9 ingredients in medium bowl. Add to chocolate mixture. Stir until just moistened. Turn into greased 9 x 5 x 3 inch (22 x 12.5 x 7.5 cm) loaf pan. Bake in 350°F (175°C) oven for 60 to 70 minutes until wooden pick inserted in center comes out clean. Let stand in pan for 15 minutes. Turn out onto wire rack to cool. Makes 1 loaf. Cuts into 18 slices.

1 slice: 225 Calories; 9.7 g Total Fat; 194 mg Sodium; 4 g Protein; 33 g Carbohydrate; 1 g Dietary Fiber

Pictured on page 22 and page 23.

Swedish Tea Ring, this page

Swedish Tea Ring

Keep your presentation of this picturesque loaf simple—just a large serving plate and some colorful ribbon.

Warm water	1/2 cup	125 mL
Granulated sugar	1 tbsp.	15 mL
Envelope of active dry yeast (or 2 1/2 tsp., 12 mL, bulk)	1/4 oz.	8 g
Large egg, fork-beaten	1	1
Warm milk	1/2 cup	125 mL
Salt	1/2 tsp.	2 mL
Cooking oil	3 tbsp.	50 mL
Granulated sugar	2 tbsp.	30 mL
All-purpose flour, approximately	4 cups	1 L
FILLING		
Hard margarine (or butter), softened	2 tbsp.	30 mL
Brown sugar, packed	1/4 cup	60 mL
Granulated sugar	1/4 cup	60 mL
Chopped glazed cherries	1/4 cup	60 mL
Raisins	1/4 cup	60 mL
ICING		
Icing (confectioner's) sugar	2/3 cup	150 mL
Milk	4 tsp.	20 mL
Corn syrup	1 tsp.	5 mL
Vanilla	1/4 tsp.	1 mL
Slivered almonds, toasted (see Note)	1/2 cup	125 mL

Stir warm water and first amount of sugar in small bowl. Sprinkle with yeast. Let stand for 10 minutes. Stir to dissolve yeast.

Combine egg, warm milk, salt, cooking oil and second amount of sugar in large bowl. Add yeast mixture. Stir. Gradually mix in flour until dough leaves sides of bowl. Turn out onto lightly floured surface. Knead until smooth and elastic. Cover with tea towel. Let stand in oven with light on and door closed for about 1 hour until doubled in bulk. Punch dough down. Roll dough into 18 x 10 inch (45 x 25 cm) rectangle.

Filling: Spread rectangle with margarine.

Stir both sugars in small bowl. Sprinkle over margarine. Sprinkle with cherries and raisins. Roll up, jelly-roll style, starting at long side. Moisten edges. Pinch to seal. Place on greased baking sheet, seam side down. Shape into circle, slipping ends inside each other, pinching to seal. Stretch to make slightly larger circle. Using scissors, make cuts from outside edge to within about 1 inch (2.5 cm) of center, 1 inch (2.5 cm) apart. Turn each cut wedge on its side, all in same direction allowing them to overlap. Spray with non-stick cooking spray. Cover with tea towel. Let stand in oven with light on and door closed for about 40 minutes until doubled in size. Bake in 375°F (190°C) oven for about 30 minutes. Let stand for 10 minutes. Transfer to wire rack.

Icing: Combine first 4 ingredients in small bowl. Drizzle over ring.

Sprinkle with almonds. Cuts into 14 slices.

1 slice: 299 Calories; 7.6 g Total Fat; 118 mg Sodium; 6 g Protein; 52 g Carbohydrate; 2 g Dietary Fiber

Pictured above.

Note: To toast nuts or seeds, place in single layer in ungreased shallow pan. Bake in 350°F (175°C) oven for 5 to 10 minutes, stirring or shaking often, until desired doneness.

Cherry Coffee Cake

Bake this pretty cake in a disposable foil pan—your recipient will appreciate not having to remember to return it.

Hard margarine (or butter), softened	1/2 cup	125 mL
Granulated sugar	1 cup	250 mL
Large eggs	3	3
Vanilla	1 tsp.	5 mL
All-purpose flour	1 3/4 cups	425 mL
Baking powder	1 1/2 tsp.	7 mL
Salt	1/2 tsp.	2 mL
Milk	1/4 cup	60 mL
Can of cherry pie filling	19 oz.	540 mL
TOPPING		
Hard margarine (or butter)	3 tbsp.	50 mL
Brown sugar, packed	1/2 cup	125 mL
All-purpose flour	1/4 cup	60 mL
Ground cinnamon	1 tsp.	5 mL

Cream margarine and sugar together in large bowl. Beat in eggs, 1 at a time. Add vanilla. Beat.

Add flour, baking powder, salt and milk. Stir until just moistened. Pour 2 cups (500 mL) batter into greased 9 x 13 inch (22 x 33 cm) pan.

Drop tiny spoonfuls of cherry filling here and there over top. Drop dabs of remaining batter over cherry filling.

Topping: Melt margarine in small saucepan. Add brown sugar, flour and cinnamon. Mix. Sprinkle over batter. Bake in 350°F (175°C) oven for about 45 minutes. Cuts into 15 pieces.

1 piece: 289 Calories; 10.1 g Total Fat; 241 mg Sodium; 4 g Protein; 47 g Carbohydrate; 1 g Dietary Fiber

Pictured on page 51.

Apricot Coffee Cake

Shows beautifully! Slices nicely! Tastes wonderful! Blend of apricot and almond flavors.

All-purpose flour	1 3/4 cups	425 mL
Granulated sugar	1/3 cup	75 mL
Hard margarine (or butter), softened	2/3 cup	150 mL
Large egg	1	1
Light cream cheese, softened	8 oz.	250 g
Granulated sugar	1/2 cup	125 mL
Light sour cream	1 cup	250 mL
All-purpose flour	2 tbsp.	30 mL
Baking powder	1/2 tsp.	2 mL
Salt	1/2 tsp.	2 mL
Almond flavoring	1 tsp.	5 mL
Can of apricots, drained	14 oz.	398 mL
Sliced almonds	1/3 cup	75 mL

Combine first amounts of flour, sugar and margarine in medium bowl until crumbly. Reserve 3/4 cup (175 mL) crumb mixture. Press remainder in bottom of greased 9 inch (22 cm) springform pan.

Beat egg, cream cheese and second amount of sugar in large bowl. Mix in sour cream. Add second amount of flour, baking powder, salt and almond flavoring. Mix. Pour and spread over crust.

Arrange about 7 apricot halves, cut side down, around outside edge of pan and about 5 in middle. Sprinkle with reserved crumbs. Sprinkle with almonds. Bake in 350°F (175°C) oven for 90 minutes until set and well browned. Let stand for 20 minutes to serve warm, or longer to serve at room temperature. Cuts into 10 pieces.

1 piece: 391 Calories; 22.2 g Total Fat; 482 mg Sodium; 7 g Protein; 42 g Carbohydrate; 2 g Dietary Fiber

Pictured on page 51.

Top Right: Apricot Coffee Cake, above
Center: Easiest Cinnamon Treats, page 45
Bottom Right: Cherry Coffee Cake, this page

Center: Sour Cream Coffee Cake, below

Left and Right: Raspberry Coffee Cake, below

Sour Cream Coffee Cake

The streusel mix creates a marbling throughout this cake. Dark, dense, moist and delicious.

Hard margarine (or butter), softened	1/2 cup	125 mL
Granulated sugar	1 1/4 cups	300 mL
Large eggs	2	2
Vanilla	1 tsp.	5 mL
Sour cream	1 cup	250 mL
All-purpose flour	1 3/4 cups	425 mL
Baking powder	1 1/2 tsp.	7 mL
Baking soda	1/2 tsp.	2 mL
Salt	1/4 tsp.	1 mL
STREUSEL MIX		
Brown sugar, packed	1/3 cup	75 mL
Chopped pecans (or walnuts)	3/4 cup	175 mL
Ground cinnamon	1 tsp.	5 mL

Cream margarine and sugar together in large bowl. Beat in eggs, 1 at a time. Add vanilla and sour cream. Beat.

Add flour, baking powder, baking soda and salt. Stir just until moistened.

Streusel Mix: Combine brown sugar, pecans and cinnamon in small bowl. Sprinkle 1/2 into bottom of well-greased 12 cup (3 L) bundt pan. Spoon 1/2 of batter over top. Sprinkle second 1/2 of streusel mix over batter. Spoon remaining batter here and there, spreading as best you can. Bake in 350°F (175°C) oven for about 45 minutes. Wooden pick inserted in center should come out clean. Let stand in pan for 10 minutes. Turn out onto wire rack to cool. Cuts into 16 pieces.

1 piece: 261 Calories; 12.9 g Total Fat; 199 mg Sodium; 3 g Protein; 34 g Carbohydrate; 1 g Dietary Fiber

Pictured above.

Raspberry Coffee Cake

The cake rises to enclose most of the raspberries, leaving a few peeking through. Good served warm or at room temperature.

All-purpose flour	1 2/3 cups	400 mL
Granulated sugar	3/4 cup	175 mL
Baking powder	1 tbsp.	15 mL
Salt	1/4 tsp.	1 mL
Hard margarine (or butter)	1/3 cup	75 mL
Large egg, fork-beaten	1	1
Milk	1 cup	250 mL
Vanilla	1 tsp.	5 mL
Frozen whole raspberries	1 1/2 cups	375 mL
TOPPING		
Brown sugar, packed	1/2 cup	125 mL
Ground cinnamon	3/4 tsp.	4 mL

Combine flour, sugar, baking powder and salt in large bowl. Cut in margarine until crumbly.

Add egg, milk and vanilla. Stir until just moistened. Turn into greased 9 x 9 inch (22 x 22 cm) pan.

Sprinkle with raspberries.

Topping: Combine brown sugar and cinnamon in small bowl. Sprinkle over raspberries. Bake in 350°F (175°C) oven for about 50 minutes. Wooden pick inserted in center should come out clean. Cut into 9 pieces.

1 piece: 303 Calories; 8.4 g Total Fat; 300 mg Sodium; 4 g Protein; 54 g Carbohydrate; 2 g Dietary Fiber

Pictured above.

Candy

When you want to "wow" people with your kitchen finesse, candy is the gift to give (and they don't need to know how easy it was!). Create an eye-catching tray of luscious fudge or a box of melt-in-your-mouth truffles made with the smoothest chocolate. These candies are so good everyone will want some, so be sure and make enough for several gifts!

White Crème Fudge, Choco Peanut Fudge, page 60

Rum Balls

A classic "sweet" for Christmas gift-giving.

Chocolate cake mix (1 layer size)	1	1
Cocoa, sifted	2 tbsp.	30 mL
Brown sugar, packed	1/4 cup	60 mL
Apricot jam	1/4 cup	60 mL
Boiling water	1 tbsp.	15 mL
Dark rum	2 tbsp.	30 mL
Chocolate sprinkles	1/2 - 3/4 cup	125 - 175 mL

Prepare and bake cake mix according to package directions. Cool. Partially freeze. Crumble into large bowl.

Add cocoa and brown sugar. Mix.

Combine jam, boiling water and rum in small cup. Add to cake mixture. Stir well. Shape into balls, using 1 1/2 tbsp. (25 mL) cake mixture.

Roll each ball in chocolate sprinkles. Chill. Makes 24 rum balls.

1 rum ball: 78 Calories; 2.1 g Total Fat; 90 mg Sodium; 1 g Protein; 15 g Carbohydrate; trace Dietary Fiber

Pictured on page 54.

Photo Legend previous page:
Bottom Left: Rum Balls, above
Top Left: Strawberry Divinity, page 57
Top Center: Coffee Fudge, page 57
Top Right: Sucre à la Crème, this page
Bottom Right: Truffles, this page

Sucre à la Crème

This fudge is smooth and rich. Similar to maple sugar candy. Melts in your mouth!

Brown sugar, packed	2 cups	500 mL
Whipping cream	3/4 cup	175 mL
Butter (not margarine)	6 tbsp.	100 mL
Vanilla (or maple flavoring)	1/4 tsp.	1 mL
Icing (confectioner's) sugar	1 1/2 cups	375 mL
Chopped pecans (or walnuts), optional	1/2 cup	125 mL

Combine brown sugar, whipping cream and butter in large heavy saucepan. Heat and stir until boiling. Reduce heat. Simmer for 15 minutes. Remove from heat.

Add vanilla, icing sugar and pecans. Mix. Spread in ungreased 8 × 8 inch (20 × 20 cm) pan. Cool to room temperature. Cuts into 36 pieces.

1 piece: 102 Calories; 3.6 g Total Fat; 30 mg Sodium; trace Protein; 18 g Carbohydrate; 0 g Dietary Fiber

Variation: When mixture is just mixed and still warm, spoonfuls can be pressed into greased candy molds to form candies. If you try this, only do half a recipe at a time, so you don't end up with half a saucepan of solidified candy.

Pictured on page 55.

Truffles

A nice solid truffle that will travel well in a gift box or even a gift bag. Roll some in each of the suggested coatings.

Semisweet chocolate chips	2 cups	500 mL
Milk chocolate chips	2 cups	500 mL
Whipping cream	2/3 cup	150 mL
Vanilla	1 tsp.	5 mL
COATING (Choose one)		
Cocoa, sifted if lumpy	7 tbsp.	115 mL
Plain coconut	7 tbsp.	115 mL
Fine coconut, toasted	7 tbsp.	115 mL

Combine both chocolate chips, whipping cream and vanilla in large heavy saucepan. Heat and stir on medium-low until smooth. Remove from heat. Cool to room temperature. Chill until firm. Makes 2 lbs. (900 g). Shape into balls, using 1 tsp. (5 mL) each.

Coating: Roll each ball in desired coating. Makes about 72 truffles.

1 truffle with cocoa coating: 59 Calories; 3.9 g Total Fat; 6 mg Sodium; 1 g Protein; 7 g Carbohydrate; 1 g Dietary Fiber

Pictured on page 3 and page 55.

Strawberry Divinity

Delicate both in flavor and color.
Raspberry may be used instead of strawberry.

Granulated sugar	3 cups	750 mL
Hot water	3/4 cup	175 mL
White corn syrup	3/4 cup	175 mL
Egg whites (large), room temperature	2	2
Package of strawberry-flavored gelatin (jelly powder)	3 oz.	85 g
Vanilla	1 tsp.	5 mL
Finely chopped walnuts (or pecans)	1/2 cup	125 mL

Combine sugar, hot water and corn syrup in 3 quart (3 L) heavy saucepan. Heat and stir on medium until sugar is dissolved and mixture starts to boil. Boil slowly for about 30 minutes, without stirring, until hard ball stage (250° to 265°F, 121° to 129°C) on candy thermometer or until small amount dropped into very cold water forms a rigid ball that is barely pliable. Remove from heat.

Beat egg whites in large bowl until soft peaks form. Sprinkle with gelatin. Beat until stiff and gelatin is dissolved. Pour hot syrup mixture into egg whites, in a thin steady stream, while beating. Beat until mixture begins to hold its shape.

Stir in vanilla and walnuts. Pour into greased 9 x 9 inch (22 x 22 cm) pan. Cool. Makes about 2 1/4 lbs. (1 kg). Cuts into eighty-one 1 inch (2.5 cm) squares.

1 square: 49 Calories; 1 g Total Fat; 8 mg Sodium; trace Protein;
11 g Carbohydrate; trace Dietary Fiber

Pictured on page 2 and page 54.

Pictured on page 2 and page 54.

TIP

To take the guesswork out of candy-making, the purchase of a candy thermometer is a good investment. They are available at kitchen specialty and craft stores. However, if you don't own a candy thermometer, the cold water test, stated in the recipes in this section, is reliable. It's a good idea to use both tests.

Coffee Fudge

The perfect gift for someone who likes chocolate and coffee.

Granulated sugar	2 cups	500 mL
Milk	1/2 cup	125 mL
Instant coffee granules	1 tbsp.	15 mL
Corn syrup	1 tbsp.	15 mL
Hard margarine (or butter)	1 tbsp.	15 mL
Vanilla	1/2 tsp.	2 mL

Combine first 5 ingredients in 3 quart (3 L) heavy saucepan. Heat and stir on medium-high until sugar is dissolved and mixture starts to boil. Cover. Cook for about 3 minutes until steam washes down any crystals on inside of pan. Remove cover. Boil slowly for about 30 minutes, without stirring, until mixture reaches soft ball stage (234° to 240°F, 112° to 116°C) on candy thermometer or until small amount dropped into very cold water forms a soft ball that flattens of its own accord when removed. Remove from heat. Cool until you can hold your hand on bottom of saucepan.

Add vanilla. Beat until thickened. Pour into greased 9 x 5 x 3 inch (22 x 12.5 x 7.5 cm) pan. Cool. Cuts into 30 pieces.

1 piece: 75 Calories; 0.5 g Total Fat; 9 mg Sodium; trace Protein;
18 g Carbohydrate; 0 g Dietary Fiber

Pictured on page 3 and page 55.

Pictured on page 3 and page 55.

Caramels

Soft, chewy texture. Wrap individually to keep them separate—and so they'll last longer!

Granulated sugar	2 cups	500 mL
Hard margarine (or butter)	3/4 cup	175 mL
Whipping cream	2 cups	500 mL
Corn syrup	1 3/4 cups	425 mL
Vanilla	1 tsp.	5 mL

Combine sugar, margarine, whipping cream and corn syrup in large saucepan. Heat and stir until mixture just starts to boil and sugar is discolored. Boil slowly, for about 20 minutes, stirring occasionally, until mixture reaches firm ball stage (242° to 248°F, 116° to 120°C) on candy thermometer or until a small amount dropped into very cold water forms a firm but pliable ball. Remove from heat.

Add vanilla. Beat until thickened. Pour into greased 9 x 9 inch (22 x 22 cm) pan. Cool. Makes 1 lb. (454 g). Cuts into about eighty 1 inch (2.5 cm) caramels.

1 caramel: 77 Calories; 3.8 g Total Fat; 33 mg Sodium; trace Protein;
11 g Carbohydrate; 0 g Dietary Fiber

Pictured on page 59.

Pictured on page 59.

How To

Pearl Box

Papier-mâché boxes are available at craft stores in all shapes and sizes and for every occasion. Whether you give a heart-shaped box or one shaped like a bird house, the choice is yours.

Materials: Papier-mâché box, roll of craft paper (or newspaper), spray paint, glue gun, spool of miniature strung pearls, ice pick (or nail punch), 26-gauge wire, wire cutters, package of larger bead pearls.

1. Place papier-mâché box on craft paper to protect table or counter. Spray paint box, both inside and out. Let dry according to manufacturer's instructions. Apply second coat if necessary. Let dry according to manufacturer's instructions.

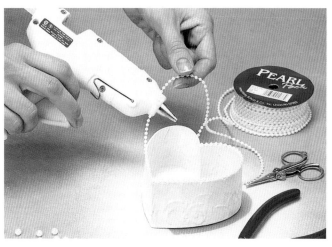

2. Make thin line of glue, 1 inch (2.5 cm) at a time, on top edge of box. Apply string of pearls, a section at a time. Poke holes in sides of box with ice pick.

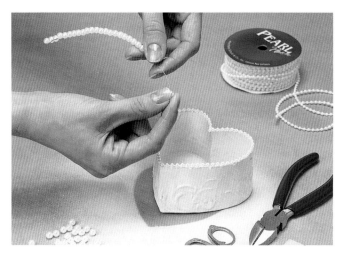

3. Cut wire to desired length for handle. Bend up one end about 1 inch (2.5 cm) so pearls don't fall off. String with larger bead pearls.

4. Attach handle of pearls to box by threading ends of wire through holes and twisting tight. Trim wire with wire cutters.

How To

Paper Doily Cones

This is a pretty holder for candies and it's easy to make in minutes.

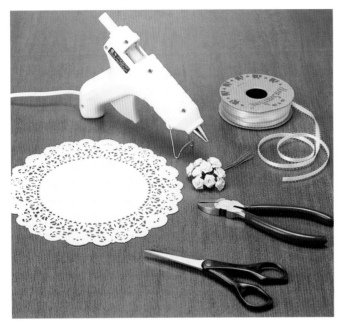

Materials: Scissors, paper doily, glue gun, ribbon, embellishments.

1. Cut doily in half. Roll one half into a cone. Make a thin line of glue along underside of one edge. Press sides together.

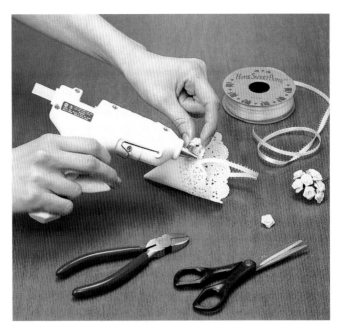

2. Cut ribbon to desired length. Attach to cone at open end with glue gun to make handle. Glue appropriate embellishment onto edge of ribbon where attached to doily.

Caramels, page 57.

Choco Peanut Fudge

This is a soft, creamy fudge so place in a sturdy container for giving. A perfect blend of chocolate and peanut flavors.

Granulated sugar	2 cups	500 mL
Cocoa, sifted	1/3 cup	75 mL
Salt	1/8 tsp.	0.5 mL
Corn syrup	2 tbsp.	30 mL
Hard margarine (or butter)	2 tbsp.	30 mL
Milk	3/4 cup	175 mL
Smooth peanut butter	1/3 cup	75 mL
Chopped peanuts (or walnuts)	1/2 cup	125 mL

Combine first 6 ingredients in large heavy saucepan. Heat and stir on medium until mixture comes to a boil. Boil slowly for about 30 minutes, without stirring, until mixture reaches soft ball stage (234° to 240°F, 112° to 116°C) on candy thermometer or until small amount dropped into very cold water forms a soft ball that flattens of its own accord when removed. Cool, without stirring, until you can hold your hand on bottom of saucepan.

Add peanut butter and peanuts. Beat with spoon until it loses its shine and pulls away from sides of pan. Pour into greased 8 x 8 inch (20 x 20 cm) pan. Chill until firm. Makes 1 1/2 lbs. (680 g). Cuts into 36 squares.

1 square: 85 Calories; 3.1 g Total Fat; 32 mg Sodium; 1 g Protein; 14 g Carbohydrate; trace Dietary Fiber

Pictured on front cover, on back cover and on page 53.

White Crème Fudge

Marshmallow crème adds a definite creaminess to this rich, sweet fudge. Fluffy and high in appearance.

Granulated sugar	2 cups	500 mL
Half-and-half cream (or evaporated milk)	2/3 cup	150 mL
Hard margarine (or butter)	1/4 cup	60 mL
Corn syrup	1 tbsp.	15 mL
White chocolate baking squares (1 oz., 28 g, each), cut up	8	8
Jar of marshmallow crème	7 oz.	200 g
Quartered glazed cherries	1/4 cup	60 mL

Combine sugar, cream, margarine and corn syrup in large heavy saucepan. Heat and stir on medium-low until mixture comes to a boil. Boil slowly for about 30 minutes, without stirring, until mixture reaches soft ball stage (234° to 240°F, 112° to 116°C) on candy thermometer or until small amount dropped into very cold water forms a soft ball that flattens of its own accord when removed. Remove from heat.

Add chocolate and marshmallow crème. Stir until chocolate is melted and mixture is smooth.

Stir in cherries. Pour into greased 8 x 8 inch (20 x 20 cm) pan. Chill until firm. Makes about 2 lbs. (900 g). Cuts into 36 pieces.

1 piece: 120 Calories; 3.7 g Total Fat; 27 mg Sodium; 1 g Protein; 22 g Carbohydrate; trace Dietary Fiber

Pictured on front cover and on page 53.

Dark Popcorn Balls

Sticky and sweet. Wrap individually for gift-giving.

Popped corn (about 1/2 cup, 125 mL, kernels unpopped)	12 cups	3 L
Candy-coated chocolate candy (such as M & M's)	1 cup	250 mL
Peanuts	2 cups	500 mL
Hard margarine (or butter), melted	1 cup	250 mL
Brown sugar, packed	2 cups	500 mL
Fancy (mild) molasses	1/2 cup	125 mL
Salt	1/4 tsp.	1 mL
Milk	1/2 cup	125 mL
Baking soda	1/2 tsp.	2 mL

Combine popped corn, chocolate candy, peanuts and margarine in large bowl or roaster.

Combine brown sugar, molasses, salt and milk in large heavy saucepan. Heat and stir until brown sugar is dissolved and mixture just starts to boil. Boil for about 3 1/2 minutes, without stirring, until mixture reaches hard ball stage (250° to 265°F, 121° to 129°C) on candy thermometer or until small amount dropped into very cold water forms a rigid ball that is barely pliable. Remove from heat.

Stir in baking soda. Pour over popcorn mixture. Toss until all pieces are well coated. When cool enough to handle, shape into 2 1/2 inch (6.3 cm) balls, using lightly greased hands. Makes about 24 balls.

1 ball: 299 Calories; 16.6 g Total Fat; 272 mg Sodium; 4 g Protein; 36 g Carbohydrate; 2 g Dietary Fiber

Pictured below.

Pink Popcorn Balls

Be prepared to work fast as soon as you pour the marshmallow mixture over the popped corn.

Hard margarine (or butter)	1/4 cup	60 mL
Miniature white marshmallows, lightly packed	4 cups	1 L
Package of wild raspberry-flavored (or other red-colored) gelatin (jelly powder)	3 oz.	85 g
Popped corn (about 1/2 cup, 125 mL, kernels unpopped)	12 cups	3 L

Melt margarine in large saucepan. Add marshmallows. Heat and stir on medium until melted.

Add gelatin. Stir to dissolve.

Pour marshmallow mixture over popped corn in large bowl or roaster. Stir until well coated. Shape into 12 balls, using greased hands. Wrap individually in plastic wrap or plastic bags to store. Makes 12 balls.

1 ball: 147 Calories; 4.4 g Total Fat; 73 mg Sodium; 2 g Protein; 26 g Carbohydrate; 1 g Dietary Fiber

Pictured below.

Variation: To make another color, simply use a different colored gelatin.

Dark Popcorn Balls, this page
Pink Popcorn Balls, above

Cream Cheese Mints, below   Fudgey Chocolate Mints, below   After-Dinner Mints, page 63

Cream Cheese Mints

Showy and colorful. Smooth, creamy candies
with a very mild mint flavor.

Cream cheese, softened	4 oz.	125 g
Icing (confectioner's) sugar	3 1/2 cups	875 mL
Peppermint flavoring (see Note)	1/8 tsp.	0.5 mL
Red, green, yellow food coloring		
Granulated sugar	3/4 cup	175 mL

Combine cream cheese, icing sugar and peppermint flavoring in large bowl. Stir until well mixed. Divide into 4 portions.

Place 1 portion in small bowl. Add 1 drop of red food coloring. Knead until color is evenly distributed. Knead in more icing sugar if dough is sticky. Repeat with remaining dough and colors, leaving 1 portion white. Roll into small 1/2 inch (12 mm) balls.

Roll balls in sugar. Press into small molds or press down with bottom of glass, thumb or fork. Immediately remove to waxed paper to dry. Chill. Store in airtight container. Makes about 146 mints.

1 mint: 19 Calories; 0.3 g Total Fat; 3 mg Sodium; trace Protein;
4 g Carbohydrate; 0 g Dietary Fiber

Pictured above.

Note: You may add a few more drops of peppermint to dough to desired mintiness.

Fudgey Chocolate Mints

An all-chocolate creamy, don't-have-to-
wait-until-after-eight mint.

Milk chocolate chips	1 cup	250 mL
Semisweet chocolate chips	2 cups	500 mL
Can of sweetened condensed milk	11 oz.	300 mL
Hard margarine (or butter)	2 tbsp.	30 mL
Vanilla	1 tsp.	5 mL
Peppermint flavoring (see Note)	1/8 tsp.	0.5 mL

Combine all 6 ingredients in heavy 2 quart (2 L) saucepan. Heat, stirring often, on medium-low until chocolate is melted and mixture is smooth. Pour into greased 9 x 9 inch (22 x 22 cm) pan. Cool. Makes a scant 2 lbs. (900 g). Cuts into 144, 3/4 inch (2 cm) mints.

1 mint: 28 Calories; 1.5 g Total Fat; 7 mg Sodium; trace Protein;
4 g Carbohydrate; trace Dietary Fiber

Pictured above.

Note: You may add a few more drops of peppermint to dough to desired mintiness.

Variation: For individual candies, drop by teaspoonfuls onto waxed paper. If chocolate mixture becomes hard, reheat on low, stirring often until desired consistency.

After-Dinner Mints

Small melt-in-your-mouth mints.

Water	1/2 cup	125 mL
Envelopes of unflavored gelatin (1/4 oz., 7 g, each)	3	3
Peppermint flavoring	1 1/2 tsp.	7 mL
Icing (confectioner's) sugar	2 cups	500 mL
Baking powder	1/4 tsp.	1 mL
Icing (confectioner's) sugar	4 cups	1 L

Pour water into medium saucepan. Sprinkle gelatin over top. Let stand for 2 minutes. Heat and stir on medium until gelatin dissolves. Remove from heat.

Add peppermint flavoring, first amount of icing sugar and baking powder. Mix well.

Add second amount of icing sugar. Mix and work with hands. It will be sticky. Turn out onto lightly floured counter. Knead dough until creamy. Divide into 4 equal portions. Keep 3 portions of dough covered with plastic wrap. Roll 1 portion into long cigar shape ropes, about 1/2 inch (12 mm) in diameter. Cut into 1/2 inch (12 mm) pieces with scissors or knife. Mints look neater when cut with scissors. Place on waxed paper-lined baking sheet in single layer. Let stand for 1 hour. Repeat with remaining portions. Store in plastic bags. Makes about 1 lb. (454 g), enough for 168 mints.

1 mint: 18 Calories; 0 g Total Fat; 1 mg Sodium; trace Protein;
5 g Carbohydrate; 0 g Dietary Fiber

Pictured on page 62.

Quick Marshmallows

Delectable cubes of fluff.

Water	1 1/2 cups	375 mL
Envelopes of unflavored gelatin (1/4 oz., 7 g, each)	3	3
Granulated sugar	2 1/4 cups	550 mL
Vanilla	1 tsp.	5 mL
Icing (confectioner's) sugar	1 tbsp.	15 mL

Pour water into medium saucepan. Sprinkle gelatin over top. Let stand for 1 minute.

Add sugar and vanilla. Heat and stir on medium until gelatin and sugar are dissolved. Remove from heat. Cool until you can almost hold your hand on side of saucepan. Beat on high for 15 to 20 minutes until stiff peaks form.

Sift icing sugar into 9 x 13 inch (22 x 33 cm) pan until bottom is coated. Turn marshmallow mixture into pan. Chill. Cuts into 77 squares.

1 square: 25 Calories; 0 g Total Fat; 1 mg Sodium; trace Protein;
6 g Carbohydrate; 0 g Dietary Fiber

Variation: Omit icing sugar. Divide 1/2 cup (125 mL) medium coconut into 4 small jars. Add a few drops of a different color food coloring to each. Shake well. Spread coconut on waxed paper, 1 color at a time. Roll marshmallows in coconut. Color more coconut if needed.

Variation: Omit icing sugar. Place 1/2 cup (125 mL) medium coconut in pie plate. Bake in 350°F (175°C) oven for 2 to 5 minutes, stirring once or twice, until toasted and golden. Cool thoroughly. Coat marshmallows with toasted coconut. Toast more coconut if needed.

Pictured below.

Quick Marshmallows, this page

Hot Choco Coffee Mix, page 128

How To

Dipping Chocolate

Chocolate is decadent, there's no doubt about that.

Either chocolate baking squares or chocolate melting wafers (available at most grocery stores or craft stores) can be used for dipping. Whenever working with melted chocolate, be careful not to get any water in the chocolate as it will seize or go lumpy.

Chocolate can be melted in one of three ways:

1. Place broken chocolate in a heavy saucepan on lowest heat. Stir constantly until smooth. Remove from heat immediately.

2. Place broken chocolate in top portion of double boiler over hot (not boiling) water that is not touching the bottom of upper pan. Stir constantly until smooth. Remove from heat immediately.

3. Chocolate can also be melted in the microwave oven. Place broken chocolate in a microwave-safe bowl. Microwave on medium (50%) for 1 minute. Stir gently. Continue to heat, if needed, in increasingly shorter time increments until mostly melted. Remove and stir until smooth.

Dip item in chocolate and set on baking sheet or other clean surface. Drizzle other types of chocolate over the first coat once set for a decorative effect. Don't store chocolate in the refrigerator unless room temperature is above 75°F (25°C). Chilled or frozen chocolate should be tightly wrapped to prevent texture changes due to condensation.

Turn dried fruits, candies and even coffee beans into a truly luscious gift with a coating of milk, dark, white or colored chocolate.

Pictured on page 65

Dipping Chocolate, this page

Clockwise from top:

Hazelnut cookies, vanilla wafers, dried blueberries, candy stick, dried apricots, chocolate wafers, Swedish jelly berries, caramel popcorn, dried cranberries, pretzels, dried papaya, coffee beans (center)

Nutty Brittle

Loads of nuts! Typical hard brittle but the flavors of the three nuts are distinct.

Granulated sugar	1 1/2 cups	375 mL
White corn syrup	1 cup	250 mL
Water	1/2 cup	125 mL
Salt	1/4 tsp.	1 mL
Hard margarine (or butter)	2 tbsp.	30 mL
Vanilla	2 tsp.	10 mL
Baking soda	1 tsp.	5 mL
Whole almonds, with skin	1 cup	250 mL
Cashews	1 cup	250 mL
Dry roasted peanuts	1 cup	250 mL

Combine sugar, corn syrup, water and salt in heavy medium saucepan. Heat and stir on medium until sugar is dissolved and mixture starts to boil. Boil, stirring occasionally, for about 15 minutes until hard-crack stage (300° to 310°F, 149° to 154°C) on candy thermometer or until small amount dropped into very cold water separates into hard, brittle threads. Remove from heat.

Add margarine, vanilla, baking soda, almonds, cashews and peanuts. Mix well. Immediately pour onto large greased baking sheet. Quickly lift and stretch nut mixture with forks into about 14 x 12 inch (35 x 30 cm) rectangle. Cool completely on baking sheet. Break brittle into small pieces. Store in tightly covered container. Makes 1 2/3 lbs. (734 g), about 24 (2 dozen) pieces.

1 oz. (28 g): 211 Calories; 10.2 g Total Fat; 109 mg Sodium; 4 g Protein; 29 g Carbohydrate; 1 g Dietary Fiber

Pictured on this page.

Nutty Brittle, this page   Chocolate Nut Snacks, below

Chocolate Nut Snacks

Mounds of goodness covered in lots of chocolate. Store at room temperature.

Semisweet chocolate chips	2 cups	500 mL
Ground cinnamon	1/2 tsp.	2 mL
Slivered almonds, toasted (see Note)	1 cup	250 mL
Rice Cheks cereal (or O-shaped toasted oat cereal)	1 1/2 cups	375 mL

Melt chocolate chips in large saucepan on low, stirring often. Stir in cinnamon. Remove from heat.

Add almonds and cereal. Stir until all pieces are coated. Drop by heaping teaspoonfuls onto waxed paper. Cool thoroughly. Store in layers, with waxed paper between each layer, in airtight container. Makes 19 snacks.

1 snack: 132 Calories; 8.8 g Total Fat; 20 mg Sodium; 2 g Protein; 14 g Carbohydrate; 2 g Dietary Fiber

Pictured above.

Note: To toast almonds, place in single layer in ungreased shallow baking dish. Bake in 350°F (175°C) oven for 5 to 8 minutes, watching carefully so they don't burn.

Condiments

Put a little zing in your gifts with these sauces and preserves. Match up Italian flavors with shapely pastas, or create a tangy sauce for the brother-in-law who prides himself on his barbecue skills! Adventurous friends will enjoy the unique taste of a flavored oil or vinegar, and nothing finishes off a breakfast-in-bed gift better than homemade pancake syrup, complete with bed tray and newspaper subscription.

Dilly Carrots, page 74

Basic Tomato Sauce

A fun gift for someone who is on their own for the first time. Give with a package of pasta and a Parmesan cheese shaker.

Cans of diced tomatoes (14 oz., 398 mL, each), with juice	3	3
Finely chopped onion	3/4 cup	175 mL
Granulated sugar	2 tsp.	10 mL
Dried sweet basil	1 tsp.	5 mL
Dried whole oregano	1 tsp.	5 mL
Bay leaf	1	1
Salt	1/2 tsp.	2 mL
Pepper	1/4 tsp.	1 mL
Garlic powder	1/4 tsp.	1 mL

Combine all 9 ingredients in large saucepan. Heat and stir until boiling. Reduce heat. Cover. Simmer for 1 1/2 hours, stirring often. (To thicken tomato sauce, remove cover and simmer for 45 to 60 minutes until desired consistency.) Cool. Pour into jar with tight-fitting lid. Makes 4 cups (1 L).

1/2 cup (125 mL): 42 Calories; 0.4 g Total Fat; 396 mg Sodium; 2 g Protein; 9 g Carbohydrate; 2 g Dietary Fiber

Pictured on page 68.

DIRECTIONS FOR

Basic Tomato Sauce: Refrigerate for up to 1 week or freeze for up to 6 months. To serve, scramble-fry 1 lb. (454 g) ground beef or hot sausage. Combine with sauce. Heat through. Serve over pasta. Serves 8.

Photo Legend previous page
from left to right:

Pesto, this page
Basic Tomato Sauce, above
Sweet And Sour Sauce, this page
Tenderizing Marinade, page 71
Awesome Barbecue Sauce, page 71

Pesto

Great to give frozen so that the pesto-lover in your life always has some on hand.

Fresh sweet basil, lightly packed	2 cups	500 mL
Fresh parsley	2 cups	500 mL
Garlic cloves, chopped	4	4
Slivered almonds, chopped	1/2 cup	125 mL
Olive (or cooking) oil	3/4 cup	175 mL
Grated fresh Parmesan cheese	3/4 cup	175 mL
Salt	1/8 tsp.	0.5 mL
Freshly ground pepper, sprinkle		

Process first 4 ingredients in food processor until paste-like consistency.

With motor running, gradually add olive oil through feed tube in a steady stream. Add cheese, salt and pepper. Process until combined well. Freeze in ice cube trays. Makes 1 1/2 cups (375 mL).

2 tbsp. (30 mL): 183 Calories; 18.1 g Total Fat; 150 mg Sodium; 4 g Protein; 2 g Carbohydrate; 1 g Dietary Fiber

Pictured on page 68.

Sweet And Sour Sauce

This recipe can easily be doubled for twice the gift-giving fun!

Can of tomato sauce	7 1/2 oz.	213 mL
White vinegar	1/4 cup	60 mL
Brown sugar, packed	1/3 cup	75 mL
Soy sauce	2 tbsp.	30 mL
Ground ginger	1/4 tsp.	1 mL
Garlic powder	1/4 tsp.	1 mL
Onion powder	1/4 tsp.	1 mL
Water	2 tbsp.	30 mL
Cornstarch	1 tbsp.	15 mL

Combine first 7 ingredients in medium saucepan. Heat and stir until boiling.

Stir water into cornstarch in small cup until smooth. Gradually stir into boiling mixture. Heat and stir until boiling and thickened. Pour into jar with tight-fitting lid. Makes 1 1/2 cups (375 mL).

2 tbsp. (30 mL): 34 Calories; trace Total Fat; 276 mg Sodium; 1 g Protein; 8 g Carbohydrate; trace Dietary Fiber

Pictured on page 69.

Tenderizing Marinade

*Offers a subtle "kick" that doesn't fade after grilling.
Good for lean pork loin chops and top or bottom
sirloin steaks. Will tenderize 4 to 6 pork chops
or 2 to 3 top sirloin steaks.*

Soy sauce	1/4 cup	60 mL
Freshly squeezed lime juice	2 tbsp.	30 mL
Sesame (or cooking) oil	1 tbsp.	15 mL
Liquid honey	1 tbsp.	15 mL
Garlic cloves, minced	2	2
Green onion, cut into 4 pieces	1	1
Dried crushed chilies	1 tsp.	5 mL

Process all 7 ingredients in blender until smooth. Pour into jar with tight-fitting lid. Makes 2/3 cup (150 mL).

2 tbsp. (30 mL): 47 Calories; 2.6 g Total Fat; 793 mg Sodium; 1 g Protein; 5 g Carbohydrate; trace Dietary Fiber

Pictured on page 69.

DIRECTIONS FOR
Tenderizing Marinade: Store in refrigerator for no more than 3 days. Place pork or beef in large re-sealable freezer bag. Add marinade. Seal bag. Coat meat by tipping bag back and forth. Marinate in refrigerator overnight. Grill meat, discarding bag and marinade.

Awesome Barbecue Sauce

*A nice sweet and sour flavor combination that
will please any barbecue enthusiast.*

Can of tomato paste	5 1/2 oz.	156 mL
Brown sugar, packed	1 cup	250 mL
Water	1 cup	250 mL
Fancy (mild) molasses	1/2 cup	125 mL
White vinegar	1/2 cup	125 mL
Salt	1 tsp.	5 mL
Liquid smoke	1 tsp.	5 mL
Ground ginger	3/4 tsp.	4 mL
Onion powder	1/2 tsp.	2 mL
Garlic powder	1/2 tsp.	2 mL
Water	1/2 cup	125 mL
Cornstarch	1/4 cup	60 mL

Combine first 10 ingredients in medium saucepan. Stir. Bring to a boil, stirring often.

Stir second amount of water into cornstarch in small bowl until smooth. Gradually stir into boiling mixture. Heat and stir until boiling and thickened. Cool. Pour into jars with tight-fitting lids. Keep in refrigerator. Makes 3 1/2 cups (875 mL).

2 tbsp. (30 mL): 56 Calories; 0.1 g Total Fat; 91 mg Sodium; trace Protein; 14 g Carbohydrate; trace Dietary Fiber

Pictured on page 69.

How To

Jar Toppers

Make your preserves say "gift" by taking the time to decorate the lid with fabric, tissue, screening or whatever else you have on hand. Embellishments (page 47) are limited only by your imagination.

2. Form fabric circle over lid with hand. Hold in place with rubber band. Cut ribbon to desired length. Tie around lid, hiding rubber band.

Materials: Jars of preserves, cardboard (or construction paper), pen, scissors, fabric, pinking shears (or other design-edged scissors), rubber band, ribbon, embellishments, glue gun.

1. Outline lid on cardboard. Enlarge pattern by 3 inches (7.5 cm) all around. Cut out. Trace circle pattern on wrong side of fabric. Cut out with pinking shears. (Pinking shears give a zigzag edge that doesn't fray easily and looks pretty.)

3. Attach embellishments with glue gun.

How To

Shrink Wrapping

Both shrink wrap and cellophane allow gift items to be seen, but shrink wrapping keeps the items from shifting around. Shrink wrap is available at craft stores in rolls or bags shaped for baskets with handles. It gives a professional presentation and is a cinch to use.

Materials: Gift items, basket (or container), shrink wrap, scissors, tape, blow dryer.

Arrange gift items in basket. Cut shrink wrap large enough to wrap and tape underneath basket. Blow dry according to manufacturer's instructions.

Craft Helpers

When you have the proper tools for a job, it becomes more fun and easier to accomplish. Keep the items listed below at arm's reach to simplify and encourage gift-giving.

♦ **Cellophane:** A roll of clear, colored or patterned cellophane is handy for wrapping gift baskets and awkward shapes. Colored or patterned cellophane should not come in direct contact with food as the ink could transfer. Your food item can be covered with plastic wrap first if it's not already in a bottle or jar.

♦ **Fabric pieces:** If you have scraps left over from clothes or from sewing projects, they can find a new life as jar toppers or decoupage material.

♦ **Glue gun:** Choose a low-temperature glue gun that uses small white sticks. High-temperature guns only increase the chance of burns. A glue gun is great for attaching embellishments and labels. They're inexpensive and once you have one, you'll find a lot of uses for it.

♦ **Hole punch:** Threading ribbon through a tag is easier with one of these.

♦ **Needle and thread:** You never know when you'll have to stitch fabric together or sew on an embellishment.

♦ **Paper or tissue paper:** Scraps of paper, cardboard or tissue paper in different colors can be transformed into gift tags or recipe cards. Cut out different shapes by tracing around cookie cutters or using design-edged scissors.

♦ **Pinking shears:** These scissors have a zigzag edge that's perfect for creating a basic decorative edge for paper or fabric. The advantage of cutting fabric with these is that it will fray less.

♦ **Ribbon:** With the variety of ribbon available, almost any recipe can appear festive. There's every width and color; some have wire edges that will hold a shape.

♦ **Sharp scissors (or utility knife):** Keep a pair of scissors on hand for cutting paper, fabric, twine or thin wire. Cut with a utility knife on a cutting board to save your countertop.

♦ **White glue:** This doesn't dry as fast as hot glue, but it does dry clear and can be brushed or spread flat. White glue is good for pasting paper together or for decoupage (see page 86).

♦ **Wire:** Both craft wire and florist wire are available in 16 through 28 gauge. The lower the gauge the thicker the wire. Florist wire is often sold in bundles of about 18 inches (45 cm) in length. Craft wire is often sold in rolls.

♦ **Wire cutters:** Reach for these for cutting wire and save your scissors.

Hot Pickled Peppers

What a great gift for those who love their food hot and spicy! The tiny (but very hot) Thai peppers are available either in the produce section of your grocery store or at an Asian grocery store.

Mixed hot peppers (green, red, yellow, habanero or Thai)	1 lb.	454 g
BRINE		
White vinegar	4 cups	1 L
Granulated sugar	1 1/2 cups	375 mL
Coarse (pickling) salt	4 tsp.	20 mL

Wash peppers well. Trim stems to 1/4 inch (6 mm). Gently, but firmly, pack peppers vertically into 1 hot sterilized quart (4 cup, 1 L) jar for the larger peppers or 4 half pint (1 cup, 250 mL) jars for the small Thai peppers. Do not squish peppers.

Brine: Heat vinegar, sugar and coarse salt in large saucepan until sugar and salt are dissolved. Bring to a boil. Pour over peppers to within 1/2 inch (12 mm) of top. Place sterilized metal lid on jar and screw metal band on securely. Process in boiling water bath for 10 minutes. Cool. Store for 3 weeks before using. Makes 1 quart (4 cup, 1 L) jar or 4 half pint (1 cup, 250 mL) jars.

1/4 cup (60 mL): 76 Calories; 0.2 g Total Fat; 303 mg Sodium; 2 g Protein; 19 g Carbohydrate; 1 g Dietary Fiber

Pictured on front cover.

Dilly Carrots

One of the simplest but prettiest of the pickled vegetables. This is one gift that may get left on the kitchen counter unopened!

BRINE		
Water	1 1/2 cups	375 mL
White vinegar	3 cups	750 mL
Granulated sugar	1/4 cup	60 mL
Coarse (pickling) salt	2 tbsp.	30 mL
Garlic cloves	4	4
Fresh heads of baby dill (or 1 tbsp., 15 mL, dill weed)	4	4
Dill seed	1/2 tsp.	2 mL
Hot peppers (optional)	4	4
Medium carrots, peeled and cut into 3 inch (7.5 cm) sticks	2 lbs.	900 g

Brine: Combine water, vinegar, sugar and coarse salt in large saucepan. Bring to a boil. Boil for 5 minutes.

Put 1 garlic clove, 1 fresh dill head, 1/8 tsp. (0.5 mL) dill seed and 1 hot pepper at bottom of each of 4 hot sterilized pint (2 cup, 500 mL) jars. Gently pack carrots vertically into jars. Pour brine over carrots to within 1/2 inch (12 mm) of top. Place sterilized metal lids on jars and screw metal bands on securely. Process in boiling water bath for 15 minutes. Cool. Store for 3 weeks before using. Makes 4 pint (2 cup, 500 mL) jars.

1/4 cup (60 mL): 15 Calories; 0.1 g Total Fat; 230 mg Sodium; trace Protein; 4 g Carbohydrate; 1 g Dietary Fiber

Pictured on back cover and on page 67.

Acorn Pickles

Similar in taste to bread and butter pickles only with squash instead of cucumbers.

Peeled, seeded and cubed acorn squash (about 2 medium)	6 cups	1.5 L
Red peppers, cut into strips	2	2
Sliced onion	1 1/2 cups	375 mL
Salt	1 tbsp.	15 mL
Granulated sugar	2 cups	500 mL
Brown sugar, packed	1/4 cup	60 mL
Mustard seed	1 1/2 tsp.	7 mL
Celery salt	1/2 tsp.	2 mL
White vinegar	1 1/2 cups	375 mL

Combine squash, red pepper and onion in large bowl. Sprinkle with salt. Stir gently. Let stand for 1 hour. Drain.

Combine both sugars in large pot or Dutch oven. Add mustard seed, celery salt and vinegar. Heat, stirring often, until boiling and sugar is dissolved. Add squash mixture. Stir gently. Bring to a boil. Boil for 4 minutes. Fill hot sterilized jars to within 1/2 inch (12 mm) of top. Place sterilized metal lids on jars and screw metal bands on securely. Process in boiling water bath for 10 minutes. Makes 7 half pint (1 cup, 250 mL) jars.

1/4 cup (60 mL): 88 Calories; 0.1 g Total Fat; 276 mg Sodium; 1 g Protein; 23 g Carbohydrate; 1 g Dietary Fiber

Pictured below.

Acorn Pickles, above

Refrigerator Pickles

*A sweet pickle that will last for up to
2 months in the refrigerator.*

Thinly sliced English cucumber, with peel (about 3 large)	8 cups	2 L
Thinly sliced onion	1 1/2 cups	375 mL
Sliced green pepper	1/2 cup	125 mL
BRINE		
Granulated sugar	2 cups	500 mL
White vinegar	2 cups	500 mL
Salt	1 tbsp.	15 mL
Celery seed	1 tbsp.	15 mL
Mustard seed	1 1/2 tsp.	7 mL

Place cucumber, onion and green pepper in large bowl.

Brine: Combine all 5 ingredients in large saucepan. Bring to a boil, stirring often. Boil for 3 minutes. Pour over cucumber mixture. Stir. Cool. Fill jars or plastic containers. Chill for 3 to 4 days to allow flavors to develop. Makes 6 cups (1.5 L).

1/2 cup (125 mL): 165 Calories; 0.4 g Total Fat; 593 mg Sodium; 1 g Protein; 42 g Carbohydrate; 1 g Dietary Fiber

Pictured below.

Pickled Beets And Onions

*Cover the lid with green fabric, and you have
a festive-looking gift.*

Cans of baby beets (14 oz., 398 mL, each), drained	4	4
Pickling (or pearl) onions	2 cups	500 mL
Mixed pickling spice	4 tsp.	20 mL
Water	1 cup	250 mL
White vinegar	1/2 cup	125 mL
Apple cider vinegar	3/4 cup	175 mL
Granulated sugar	1 cup	250 mL
Salt	1 tsp.	5 mL
Mustard seed	1/2 tsp.	2 mL

Place whole beets in hot sterilized jars.

Place onions in rapidly boiling water. Boil for 4 minutes. Drain. Rinse under cold running water until cool. Peel off skin. Combine with beets in jar. Sprinkle 1 tsp. (5 mL) pickling spice in each jar.

Combine water, both vinegars, sugar, salt and mustard seed in large saucepan. Bring to a boil. Boil for 3 minutes. Pour over beets and onions to within 3/4 inch (2 cm) of top. Place sterilized metal lids on jars and screw metal bands on securely. Process in boiling water bath for 15 minutes. Cool. Store for 3 weeks before using. Makes 4 pint (2 cup, 500 mL) jars.

1 pint (2 cups, 500 mL): 39 Calories; trace Total Fat; 145 mg Sodium; trace Protein; 10 g Carbohydrate; 1 g Dietary Fiber

Pictured below.

Refrigerator Pickles, above

Pickled Beets And
Onions, above

To: MY BUSDRIVER

Refrigerator Pickles

PICKLED BEETS

Creamy Basil Dressing

A must for any salad lover.

White vinegar	1/4 cup	60 mL
Light salad dressing (or mayonnaise)	2/3 cup	150 mL
Cooking oil	1/4 cup	60 mL
Granulated sugar	2 tbsp.	30 mL
Salt, sprinkle		
Pepper, sprinkle		
Chopped fresh sweet basil	1/4 cup	60 mL

Process all 7 ingredients in blender until smooth. Pour into small jar. Makes about 1 cup (250 mL).

2 tbsp. (30 mL): 136 Calories; 13.1 g Total Fat; 134 mg Sodium; trace Protein; 5 g Carbohydrate; 0 g Dietary Fiber

Pictured on this page.

Variation: Omit fresh basil. Add 2 tbsp. (30 mL) basil pesto.

Raspberry Walnut Vinaigrette

This is a perfect gift to give with a bag of fresh spinach. The walnut oil is a rare treat that makes this a very special gift.

Raspberry vinegar	1/4 cup	60 mL
Minced shallots	2 tbsp.	30 mL
Chopped fresh parsley	2 tbsp.	30 mL
Walnut oil	1 tbsp.	15 mL
Cooking oil	1 tbsp.	15 mL

Process all 5 ingredients in blender until smooth. Pour into small jar. Makes 2/3 cup (150 mL).

2 tbsp. (30 mL): 59 Calories; 5 g Total Fat; 1 mg Sodium; trace Protein; 4 g Carbohydrate; trace Dietary Fiber

Pictured on this page.

DIRECTIONS FOR

Creamy Basil Dressing and Raspberry Walnut Vinaigrette:
Store in refrigerator for up to 5 days. Shake well before using.

From left to right:

Creamy Basil Dressing, above
Raspberry Walnut Vinaigrette, above
Spinach Salad Dressing, page 77
Martini Dressing, page 77

Spinach Salad Dressing

The perfect dressing for spinach!

White vinegar	1/3 cup	75 mL
Granulated sugar	1/3 cup	75 mL
Garlic powder	1/4 tsp.	1 mL
Onion powder	1/4 tsp.	1 mL
Light salad dressing (or mayonnaise)	1/3 cup	75 mL
Cooking oil	1/3 cup	75 mL
Salt	1/4 tsp.	1 mL
Maple flavoring (optional)	1/4 tsp.	1 mL
Imitation bacon bits, crushed	1 tbsp.	15 mL

Mix all 9 ingredients well in small bowl. Pour into small jar. Makes about 1 cup (250 mL).

2 tbsp. (30 mL): 114 Calories; 8.3 g Total Fat; 139 mg Sodium; trace Protein; 10 g Carbohydrate; 0 g Dietary Fiber

Pictured on this page.

Martini Dressing

Also known as "Italian Vinaigrette." Delicious tossed with a mixture of greens and tomatoes.

Olive (or cooking) oil	2/3 cup	150 mL
White wine vinegar	6 tbsp.	100 mL
Garlic cloves, minced	6	6
Chopped fresh sweet basil	1/4 cup	60 mL
Grated Romano cheese	6 tbsp.	100 mL

Process all 5 ingredients in blender for about 1 minute. Pour into small jar. Makes 1 cup (250 mL).

2 tbsp. (30 mL): 183 Calories; 19.4 g Total Fat; 55 mg Sodium; 2 g Protein; 2 g Carbohydrate; trace Dietary Fiber

Pictured on this page.

DIRECTIONS FOR

Spinach Salad Dressing and Martini Dressing: Store in refrigerator for up to 5 days. Shake well before using.

Year-Round Chutney

A dark and rich-looking chutney with
a pleasant tang from balsamic vinegar.

Mixed dried fruit, chopped (apples, prunes, pears, apricots, peaches)	2 lbs.	900 g
Raisins	1 cup	250 mL
Medium onions, chopped	2	2
Brown sugar, packed	1 1/2 cups	375 mL
Salt	1/2 tsp.	2 mL
Ground ginger	1 tsp.	5 mL
Balsamic vinegar	3/4 cup	175 mL
Water	1 cup	250 mL
Mustard seed	1/2 tsp.	2 mL

Combine all 9 ingredients in large pot or Dutch oven. Bring to a boil. Reduce heat. Cover. Simmer for about 40 minutes, stirring occasionally. Fill hot sterilized jars to within 1/2 inch (12 mm) of top. Place sterilized metal lids on jars and screw metal bands on securely. Process in boiling water bath for 10 minutes. Cool. Makes 8 half pint (1 cup, 250 mL) jars.

2 tbsp. (30 mL): 62 Calories; 0.1 g Total Fat; 23 mg Sodium; trace Protein;
16 g Carbohydrate; 1 g Dietary Fiber

Pictured on page 79.

Rhubarb Chutney

Try this instead of applesauce the next time you serve pork.

Fresh (or frozen) rhubarb, cut into 1/2 inch (12 mm) pieces (about 7 1/2 cups, 1.9 L)	2 lbs.	900 g
Granulated sugar	3 cups	750 mL
Brown sugar, packed	1 cup	250 mL
Apple cider vinegar	2 cups	500 mL
Raisins	2 cups	500 mL
Ground cinnamon	1 1/2 tsp.	7 mL
Ground cloves	1/2 tsp.	2 mL

Combine all 7 ingredients in large pot or Dutch oven. Bring to a boil, stirring often. Reduce heat. Simmer, uncovered, for about 1 hour until thickened. Pour into hot sterilized jars to within 1/2 inch (12 mm) of top. Place sterilized metal lids on jars and screw metal bands on securely. Process in boiling water bath for 10 minutes. Cool. Makes about 5 half pint (1 cup, 250 mL) jars.

2 tbsp. (30 mL): 99 Calories; 0.1 g Total Fat; 4 mg Sodium; trace Protein;
26 g Carbohydrate; 1 g Dietary Fiber

Pictured on page 79.

Top Left: Dried Porcini Mushroom And Rosemary Oil, page 80
Top Centre: Basil Oil, page 80
Top Right: Rhubarb Chutney, above
Bottom Left: Garlic Vinegar, page 80
Bottom Centre: Year-Round Chutney, above
Bottom Right: Spicy Chili Oil, page 80

Dried Porcini Mushroom And Rosemary Oil

Perfect for an Italian stir-fry.

Cooking oil	1 cup	250 mL
Dried porcini mushrooms	1/3 cup	75 mL
Fresh sprigs rosemary (or 1 1/2 tsp., 7 mL, dried)	2	2

Combine cooking oil, mushrooms and rosemary in 2 cup (500 mL) glass measure. Place on pie plate. Bake in 300°F (150°C) oven for about 1 1/2 hours until mushrooms are golden brown. Remove to wire rack to cool for 30 minutes. Line small strainer with coffee filter or several layers of cheesecloth. Strain oil into glass jar. Oil should be clear. Cover. Chill. Makes 3/4 cup (175 mL).

2 tsp. (10 mL): 108 Calories; 12.3 g Total Fat; 0 mg Sodium; 0 g Protein; 0 g Carbohydrate; 0 g Dietary Fiber

Pictured on page 78.

Spicy Chili Oil

A quick way to add spicy Thai flavors to your stir-fry.

Cooking oil	1 cup	250 mL
Dried crushed chilies	2 tsp.	10 mL
Garlic cloves	4	4
Fresh gingerroot, cut into 1/4 inch (6 mm) slices	2	2

Place cooking oil, chilies, garlic cloves and gingerroot in 2 cup (500 mL) glass measure on pie plate. Bake in 300°F (150°C) oven for about 2 hours until garlic cloves and gingerroot are golden brown. Remove to wire rack to cool for 30 minutes. Line small strainer with coffee filter or several layers of cheesecloth. Strain oil into glass jar. Oil should be clear. Cover. Chill. Makes 7/8 cup (200 mL).

2 tsp. (10 mL): 93 Calories; 10.5 g Total Fat; 0 mg Sodium; 0 g Protein; 0 g Carbohydrate; 0 g Dietary Fiber

Pictured on page 79.

Basil Oil

This flavored oil would enhance a chicken stir-fry beautifully.

| Cooking oil | 1 cup | 250 mL |
| Fresh sweet basil leaves | 15 | 15 |

Place cooking oil and basil in 2 cup (500 mL) glass measure. Place on pie plate. Bake in 300°F (150°C) oven for about 1 1/2 hours until basil is browned. Remove to wire rack to cool for 30 minutes. Line small strainer with coffee filter or several layers of cheese cloth. Strain oil into glass jar. Oil should be clear. Cover. Chill. Makes 3/4 cup (175 mL).

2 tsp. (10 mL): 108 Calories; 12.3 g Total Fat; 0 mg Sodium; 0 g Protein; 0 g Carbohydrate; 0 g Dietary Fiber

Pictured on page 79.

Garlic Vinegar

For the garlic lovers on your list.

| Garlic cloves, minced | 3 | 3 |
| Apple cider vinegar | 2 cups | 500 mL |

Place garlic in glass jar with tight-fitting lid. Fill with cider vinegar. Cover tightly. Let stand on counter for 3 weeks before using. Strain into glass jar with tight-fitting lid. Cover tightly. Chill. Makes 2 cups (500 mL).

1 tsp. (5 mL): 1 Calorie; 0 g Total Fat; trace Sodium; 0 g Protein; trace Carbohydrate; 0 g Dietary Fiber

Pictured on page 78.

Tarragon Vinegar

Choose a tall bottle that will highlight the appearance of the tarragon suspended in the vinegar.

Sprigs of fresh tarragon (about 5 inches, 12.5 cm, each)	4	4
Whole black peppercorns	6	6
Red (or white) wine vinegar	2 cups	500 mL

Place tarragon sprigs and peppercorns in glass jar with tight-fitting lid. Fill with vinegar. Cover tightly. Let stand on counter for 3 weeks before using. Chill. Makes 2 cups (500 mL).

1 tsp. (5 mL): 1 Calorie; 0 g Total Fat; trace Sodium; 0 g Protein; trace Carbohydrate; 0 g Dietary Fiber

Pictured on back cover.

Raspberry Vinegar

Mixed with oil and sugar, this vinegar is the perfect salad dressing for baby greens. Tart with just a touch of sweetness.

Fresh (or frozen) raspberries	2 cups	500 mL
Red wine vinegar	3/4 cup	175 mL
White wine vinegar	3/4 cup	175 mL
Granulated sugar	1/2 cup	125 mL

Place raspberries, both vinegars and sugar in medium stainless steel saucepan. Bring to a boil on high. Reduce heat to medium-low. Cover. Simmer gently for 5 minutes. Cool. Chill overnight. Strain through fine sieve, pressing to extract liquid. Discard pulp. Pour liquid into glass jar with tight-fitting lid. Cover tightly. Chill. Makes 2 1/4 cups (550 mL).

1 tsp. (5 mL): 5 Calories; trace Total Fat; trace Sodium; trace Protein; 1 g Carbohydrate; trace Dietary Fiber

Pictured on back cover.

DIRECTIONS FOR

Flavored oils: Use about 1 tbsp. (15 mL) oil in your favorite stir-fry. Store unused oil in refrigerator for up to 1 month.

Orange Honey

A gift of flavored honey with bagels fresh from the bakery will certainly be welcome.

Creamed honey	1 cup	250 mL
Frozen concentrated orange juice, thawed	3 tbsp.	50 mL
Grated orange peel	1 tsp.	5 mL

Combine all 3 ingredients in small bowl. Stir until smooth. Turn into small container. Makes 1 1/3 cups (325 mL).

1 tbsp. (15 mL): 62 Calories; trace Total Fat; 1 mg Sodium; trace Protein; 17 g Carbohydrate; trace Dietary Fiber

Pictured on page 83.

RASPBERRY HONEY: Combine 1 cup (250 mL) creamed honey, 1/2 cup (125 mL) raspberry jam (or other) and 1/8 tsp. (0.5 mL) ground allspice in small bowl. Stir until smooth. Turn into small container. Makes 1 1/2 cups (375 mL).

Pictured on page 83.

MAPLE HONEY: Combine 1 cup (250 mL) creamed honey, 1 tsp. (5 mL) maple flavoring and 1/2 cup (125 mL) finely chopped walnuts in small bowl. Stir until smooth. Turn into small container. Makes 1 1/3 cups (325 mL).

Pictured on page 83.

Pancake Syrup

Wonderfully sweet with a great maple flavor. Pass the pancakes, please!

Granulated sugar	4 cups	1 L
Brown sugar, packed	1 cup	250 mL
Water	2 cups	500 mL
Salt, just a pinch		
Vanilla	1 tbsp.	15 mL
Maple flavoring	1 tbsp.	15 mL

Combine both sugars, water and salt in large saucepan. Heat on medium-high, stirring often, until boiling and sugar is dissolved. Reduce heat. Cover. Simmer for 10 minutes.

Stir in vanilla and maple flavoring. Pour into hot sterilized jars. Place sterilized metal lids on jars and screw metal bands on securely. Process in boiling water bath for 5 minutes. Makes 4 2/3 cups (1.15 L).

2 tbsp. (30 mL): 108 Calories; 0 g Total Fat; 3 mg Sodium; 0 g Protein; 28 g Carbohydrate; 0 g Dietary Fiber

Pictured on page 83.

Raspberry Syrup

No Sunday morning pancake brunch is complete without this syrup. Also great over ice cream.

Fresh (or frozen, thawed) raspberries	8 cups	2 L
Lemon juice	1 tbsp.	15 mL
Corn syrup	3/4 cup	175 mL
Granulated sugar	2 cups	500 mL

Process raspberries in blender until smooth. If seedless syrup is preferred, strain purée through a fine sieve.

Combine raspberry purée, lemon juice, corn syrup and sugar in large saucepan. Heat and stir on medium until boiling. Reduce heat. Boil gently for about 5 minutes, stirring occasionally. Pour into hot sterilized jars. Place sterilized metal lids on jars and screw metal bands on securely. Process in boiling water bath for 5 minutes. Makes 5 cups (1.25 L).

2 tbsp. (30 mL): 69 Calories; 0.1 g Total Fat; 8 mg Sodium; trace Protein; 18 g Carbohydrate; 1 g Dietary Fiber

Pictured on page 83.

BLUEBERRY SYRUP: Omit raspberries. Use same amount of fresh (or frozen, thawed) blueberries.

STRAWBERRY SYRUP: Omit raspberries. Use same amount of sliced fresh (or frozen, thawed) strawberries.

DIRECTIONS FOR
Raspberry Syrup, Blueberry Syrup or Strawberry Syrup: Store in refrigerator for up to 6 months once seal is broken.

Three-Fruit Marmalade

This marmalade would win a blue ribbon at the country fair.

Large grapefruit	1	1
Medium oranges	4	4
Medium lemons	2	2
Water, 2 times amount of fruit		
Granulated sugar, approximately	8 cups	2 L
Pouches of liquid pectin (3 oz., 85 mL, each), approximately	2	2

Peel all 3 fruits thinly, trying not to get any of the pith (white flesh). Peel pith off fruit and discard. Coarsely chop peel and fruit. Process peel and fruit, in 2 or 3 batches, in food processor until peel is evenly chopped. Measure. Place in enamel pot or roaster.

Add twice as much water as fruit mixture measurement. Stir. Let stand at room temperature for 24 hours. Bring mixture to a boil, stirring occasionally. Boil for 20 minutes. Carefully measure mixture.

Add 2/3 cup (150 mL) sugar for every 1 cup (250 mL) fruit mixture. Bring to a boil. Reduce heat. Simmer, uncovered, for 2 hours, stirring occasionally.

Add liquid pectin. Stir. Bring to a boil. Boil rapidly for 3 minutes. Fill hot sterilized jars with hot marmalade. Place sterilized metal lids on jars and screw metal bands on securely. Process in boiling water bath for 5 minutes. Makes 9 half pint (1 cup, 250 mL) jars.

2 tbsp. (30 mL): 96 Calories; trace Total Fat; 3 mg Sodium; trace Protein; 25 g Carbohydrate; trace Dietary Fiber

Pictured on page 83.

Apricot Marmalade

Make this marmalade any time of the year for teacher gifts.

Finely diced dried apricots (about 1 lb., 454 g)	3 cups	750 mL
Water	3 cups	750 mL
Reserved pineapple juice, plus water to make	1 cup	250 mL
Can of crushed pineapple, drained and juice reserved	19 oz.	540 mL
Granulated sugar	6 cups	1.5 L
Lemon juice	1/4 cup	60 mL

Soak apricots in water in large pot or Dutch oven overnight.

Add pineapple juice. Bring to a boil. Reduce heat. Simmer, uncovered, for about 1 hour, stirring occasionally.

Add pineapple, sugar and lemon juice. Heat and stir until sugar is dissolved. Simmer for about 30 minutes until mixture jells (see Tip, below). Pour into hot sterilized jars. Place sterilized metal lids on jars and screw metal bands on securely. Process in boiling water bath for 5 minutes. Chill. Makes 8 half pint (1 cup, 250 mL) jars.

1 tbsp. (15 mL): 47 Calories; trace Total Fat; trace Sodium; trace Protein; 12 g Carbohydrate; trace Dietary Fiber

Pictured on page 83.

TIP

To test for jelling, place a small plate in freezer before cooking begins. When fruit mixture has finished suggested cooking time, remove from heat and put a spoonful on cold plate. Immediately return plate to freezer and wait 2 minutes. Mixture is done when it forms a mass that moves slowly as plate is tilted. A "path" drawn through with a spoon should remain spread. If more cooking time is required, cook for another 2 minutes. Remove from heat and repeat plate test.

1. Raspberry Syrup, page 81
2. Pancake Syrup, page 81
3. Apricot Marmalade, above
4. Three-Fruit Marmalade, this page
5. Strawberry Jam, page 84
6. Raspberry Honey, page 81
7. Maple Honey, page 81
8. Orange Honey, page 81

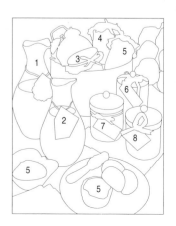

Strawberry Jam

Everybody knows that homemade jam tastes best. So this is a gift you can give to almost anybody.

Crushed strawberries	4 cups	1 L
Lemon juice	3 tbsp.	50 mL
Granulated sugar	7 cups	1.75 L
Pouch of liquid pectin	3 oz.	85 g

Place strawberries in large pot or Dutch oven. Add lemon juice and sugar. Mix well. Heat and stir on high until boiling. Boil rapidly for 1 minute.

Remove from heat. Immediately stir in liquid pectin. Skim foam off top to avoid floating fruit. Pour into hot sterilized jars. Place sterilized metal lids on jars and screw metal bands on securely. Process in boiling water bath for 5 minutes. Makes 7 half pint (1 cup, 250 mL) jars.

1 tbsp. (15 mL): 52 Calories; trace Total Fat; 1 mg Sodium; trace Protein; 14 g Carbohydrate; trace Dietary Fiber

Pictured on page 83.

TIP

To have the best-tasting jam or marmalade, always purchase fruit that is ripe, firm and not bruised. Never use overripe fruit because they contain lower levels of pectin and will not set properly.

Barbecue Sauce

This great-tasting sauce has a bite from the vinegar and a hint of smoke. Very quick and easy to make. Why not attach a barbecue basting brush and the recipe.

Chili sauce	1 1/2 cups	375 mL
White vinegar	1 cup	250 mL
Brown sugar, packed	1 cup	250 mL
Mustard seed	2 tsp.	10 mL
Celery salt	1/2 tsp.	2 mL
Worcestershire sauce	1 tbsp.	15 mL
Liquid smoke	1/2 tsp.	2 mL
Minced onion flakes	1/4 cup	60 mL
Fancy (mild) molasses	1/2 cup	125 mL
Water	1/2 cup	125 mL
Cornstarch	3 tbsp.	50 mL

Put first 9 ingredients into medium saucepan. Bring to a boil, stirring often.

Stir water into cornstarch in small cup until smooth. Gradually stir into chili sauce mixture. Heat and stir until boiling and thickened. Cool. Pour into jars with tight-fitting lids. Keep in refrigerator. Sauce can also be frozen. Makes 4 cups (1 L).

2 tbsp. (30 mL): 60 Calories; 0.1 g Total Fat; 202 mg Sodium; trace Protein; 15 g Carbohydrate; 1 g Dietary Fiber

Pictured on page 85.

Pepper Cabbage Relish

This main-course accompaniment has a sweet and sour flavor that goes great with pork.

Chopped red pepper	2 cups	500 mL
Chopped green pepper	2 cups	500 mL
Chopped, peeled tart cooking apple (such as Granny Smith)	3 cups	750 mL
Shredded red cabbage	2 cups	500 mL
Chopped banana pepper	3/4 cup	175 mL
Coarse (pickling) salt	3 tbsp.	50 mL
Granulated sugar	1 1/2 cups	375 mL
Apple cider vinegar	1 1/2 cups	375 mL
Mustard seed	1 tsp.	5 mL
Cornstarch	1 tbsp.	15 mL

Combine red and green pepper, apple, red cabbage, banana pepper and coarse salt in large bowl. Let stand for 2 hours. Drain well. Set aside.

Combine sugar, cider vinegar, mustard seed and cornstarch in large pot or Dutch oven. Bring to a boil. Reduce heat. Add pepper mixture. Stir. Simmer for about 10 minutes. Pack hot relish into hot sterilized jars to within 1/2 inch (12 mm) of top. Place sterilized metal lids on jars and screw metal bands on securely. Process in boiling water bath for 10 minutes. Cool. Makes 5 half pint (1 cup, 250 mL) jars.

2 tbsp. (30 mL): 37 Calories; 0.1 g Total Fat; 447 mg Sodium; trace Protein; 10 g Carbohydrate; trace Dietary Fiber

Pictured on page 85.

Spiced Peaches

Present your host with a ribboned jar of these savory peaches and you'll be invited back! What a nice change from a loaf cake or muffins.

Can of sliced peaches, with juice, each slice cut into 3 pieces	14 oz.	398 mL
Granulated sugar	2 tbsp.	30 mL
White vinegar	1 tbsp.	15 mL
Ground cinnamon	1/4 tsp.	1 mL
Ground ginger	1/8 tsp.	0.5 mL
Ground nutmeg	1/16 tsp.	0.5 mL
Ground cloves	1/16 tsp.	0.5 mL
Cornstarch	1/2 tsp.	2 mL

Combine all 8 ingredients in medium saucepan. Heat and stir until boiling and sugar is dissolved. Reduce heat. Simmer for about 20 minutes. Cool completely. Place in jar with tight-fitting lid or plastic container. Makes 1 1/3 cups (325 mL).

1/3 cup (75 mL): 73 Calories; 0.1 g Total Fat; 4 mg Sodium; 1 g Protein; 19 g Carbohydrate; 1 g Dietary Fiber

Pictured below.

DIRECTIONS FOR

Spiced Peaches: Serve hot or cold with any kind of meat. Store in refrigerator for up to 7 days.

Spiced Peaches, above   Barbecue Sauce, page 84   Pepper Cabbage Relish, page 84

How To

Decoupage Box

Use wrapping paper, newsprint or photocopies of family pictures as cut-outs to decoupage papier-mâché, wood, glass or clay items. Any spills from this craft activity are easily cleaned up with a damp cloth while the paste is still wet.

Materials: Scissors, small dish, instant decoupage paste, sponge brush, paper cut-outs, papier-mâché box.

1. Apply instant decoupage paste with sponge brush to back of paper cut-outs and small area of papier-mâché box.

2. Affix paper cut-out to box. Brush over cut-out, smoothing out air bubbles and wrinkles. Apply final coat of paste over entire box once all cut-outs are on.

3. This method also works well with clay pots.

Desserts

You'll be tempted to eat these desserts yourself, so make two and only give one away! This section is packed with recipes for cakes and pies, and sauces to drizzle over ice cream. Bake a chiffon or chocolate cake for a girlfriend's graduation, or a cheesecake to celebrate a parent's retirement. Your nephew will love a gift of sundae sauce, complete with his own sundae bowl, for pulling up his marks. Everyone loves dessert—it's the perfect gift!

Carrot Cake, page 94

Pineapple Chiffon Cake

A high cake with a light texture. You can't buy cakes this nice.

Cake flour	2 cups	500 mL
Granulated sugar	1 1/2 cups	375 mL
Baking powder	1 tbsp.	15 mL
Salt	1 tsp.	5 mL
Egg whites (large), room temperature	7	7
Cream of tartar	1/2 tsp.	2 mL
Reserved pineapple juice (see below)	3/4 cup	175 mL
Cooking oil	1/2 cup	125 mL
Egg yolks (large)	7	7
PINEAPPLE ICING		
Can of crushed pineapple, juice reserved	14 oz.	398 mL
Water	2 tbsp.	30 mL
Cornstarch	1 tbsp.	15 mL
Frozen whipped topping, thawed (or 2 envelopes of dessert topping, prepared with 3/4 cup, 175 mL, milk)	4 cups	1 L
Colored miniature marshmallows, for garnish	60	60
White corn syrup, for brushing		

Wash angel food pan in hot soapy water to ensure it is completely grease-free. Combine flour, sugar, baking powder and salt in sifter. Sift into large bowl. Make a well.

Beat egg whites and cream of tartar together in separate large bowl until very stiff. Set aside.

Add reserved pineapple juice, cooking oil and egg yolks to well. Beat, using same beaters, until smooth and light. Fold in egg whites, 1/4 at a time, using rubber spatula. Pour into ungreased 10 inch (25 cm) angel food tube pan. Bake in 325°F (160°C) oven for about 60 minutes. Wooden pick inserted in center should come out clean. Invert in pan to cool. When cool, remove from pan to serving plate.

Photo Legend previous page:

Top Left: Pineapple Chiffon Cake, above
Bottom Left: Apple Cake, page 91
Center: Black Forest Bake, page 91
Bottom Right: Jelly Roll, this page

Pineapple Icing: Put pineapple into medium saucepan.

Stir water into cornstarch in small cup until smooth. Gradually stir into pineapple. Heat on medium until thickened. Cool thoroughly.

Fold whipped topping into pineapple mixture. Makes 5 cups (1.25 L) icing. Ice cake.

Flatten marshmallows between fingers. Brush corn syrup on 1/2 of 1 side of each marshmallow. Arrange into 12 "flowers" on waxed paper, using 6 marshmallow "petals" for each, overlapping on the syrup. Set baking pan, half filled with water, on top for 5 minutes to glue petals together. Arrange flowers on icing. Cuts into 18 to 20 pieces.

1 piece: 272 Calories; 12.9 g Total Fat; 223 mg Sodium; 4 g Protein; 36 g Carbohydrate; trace Dietary Fiber

Pictured on page 88.

Jelly Roll

This yummy cake will remind you of angel food cake. A wonderful gift that can be frozen.

Large eggs	4	4
Granulated sugar	1 cup	250 mL
Vanilla	1/2 tsp.	2 mL
All-purpose flour	2/3 cup	150 mL
Baking powder	1 tsp.	5 mL
Salt	1/4 tsp.	1 mL
Icing (confectioner's) sugar	2 tbsp.	30 mL
Raspberry (or other) jam	1 cup	250 mL

Beat eggs in medium bowl until light colored and thickened. Add sugar and vanilla. Beat well.

Stir flour, baking powder and salt in small bowl. Add to egg mixture. Stir until moistened. Spread evenly onto greased waxed paper-lined 10 x 15 inch (25 x 38 cm) jelly roll pan. Bake in 375°F (190°C) oven for about 12 minutes. Wooden pick inserted in center should come out clean.

Turn out onto tea towel covered with sifted icing sugar. Carefully peel off waxed paper. Trim off any crisp edges.

Spread with jam. Beginning at short end, roll up, using tea towel to help raise end as you roll. Cool. Cuts into 10 slices.

1 slice: 232 Calories; 2.2 g Total Fat; 136 mg Sodium; 4 g Protein; 52 g Carbohydrate; 1 g Dietary Fiber

Pictured on page 89.

Black Forest Bake

This dessert has the three big C's—(cream) cheese, chocolate and cherry! Making this traditional layer cake in a shallow baking dish makes it so much easier to transport.

FIRST LAYER

Large eggs	2	2
Granulated sugar	1 cup	250 mL
All-purpose flour	3/4 cup	175 mL
Salt	1/8 tsp.	0.5 mL
Hard margarine (or butter)	1/2 cup	125 mL
Cocoa	1/4 cup	60 mL

SECOND LAYER

Light cream cheese	8 oz.	250 g
Granulated sugar	1 cup	250 mL
Large eggs	2	2
All-purpose flour	2 tbsp.	30 mL
Light sour cream	1/2 cup	125 mL

TOPPING

Can of cherry pie filling	19 oz.	540 mL

First Layer: Beat eggs until foamy. Add sugar, flour and salt. Stir to combine.

Melt margarine and cocoa together in small saucepan on low. Add to egg mixture. Stir. Spread in greased 9 x 13 inch (22 x 33 cm) pan.

Second Layer: Beat cream cheese and sugar together in large bowl until smooth. Beat in eggs. Add flour and sour cream. Mix. Spread over chocolate layer.

Topping: Spoon dabs of cherry filling over cream cheese layer. Marble into cheese layer with tip of knife. Bake in 350°F (175°C) oven for about 50 minutes until center is not quite firm. Cuts into 15 pieces.

1 piece: 308 Calories; 11.9 g Total Fat; 237 mg Sodium; 5 g Protein; 48 g Carbohydrate; 1 g Dietary Fiber

Pictured on page 88/89.

Apple Cake

Apple and cinnamon flavor, light and fluffy texture. Put the coffee on!

Cooking oil	1/4 cup	60 mL
Granulated sugar	1/2 cup	125 mL
Large egg	1	1
Milk	1/2 cup	125 mL
All-purpose flour	1 1/2 cups	375 mL
Baking powder	1 tbsp.	15 mL
Ground cinnamon	1/2 tsp.	2 mL
Salt	1/2 tsp.	2 mL
Peeled and chopped cooking apple (such as McIntosh), about 2 small	1 1/2 cups	375 mL

TOPPING

Brown sugar, packed	1/3 cup	75 mL
All-purpose flour	2 tbsp.	30 mL
Ground cinnamon	1/2 tsp.	2 mL
Hard margarine (or butter), melted	1 1/2 tbsp.	25 mL

Beat first 4 ingredients together in large bowl.

Stir flour, baking powder, cinnamon and salt in small bowl. Add to batter. Stir until just moistened.

Add apple. Stir. Turn into greased 8 x 8 inch (20 x 20 cm) pan.

Topping: Combine all 4 ingredients in small bowl until crumbly. Sprinkle over top. Bake in 400°F (205°C) oven for about 30 minutes until risen and apples are tender. Cuts into 9 pieces.

1 piece: 267 Calories; 9.6 g Total Fat; 299 mg Sodium; 4 g Protein; 42 g Carbohydrate; 1 g Dietary Fiber

Pictured on page 88.

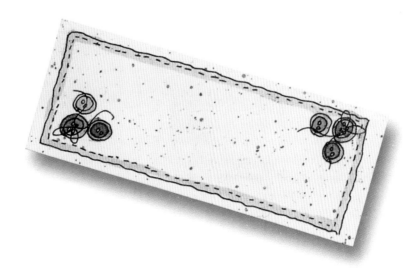

How To

Braided Holder

This braided ring dresses up a 9 x 13 inch (22 x 33 cm) casserole dish. Although the stuffing step takes time, the result is an interesting way of wrapping your gift.

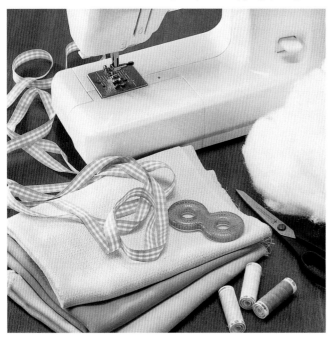

Materials: Three different colored pieces of fabric (each 10 x 60 inches, 25 x 150 cm), scissors, matching thread, sewing machine, safety pin, 1/2 pound of stuffing, pen (or unsharpened pencil), needle, ribbon, teething ring.

1. Cut strips of fabric along width, from salvage to salvage, 4 inches (10 cm) wide. With right sides facing each other, join by sewing 1/2 inch (12 mm) seam.

2. Attach safety pin to 1 edge through 1 layer of fabric. Push through inside of tube to turn inside out. Stuff a bit at a time. Using a pen will make this easier. Push stuffing to middle as you gather excess material around pen. Work on 1/2 of tube at a time, from middle to end.

3. Sew end of each tube closed. Braid tubes. To secure braid, sew each end of braid together using sewing machine. Hand sew ends of braid together, forming circle.

4. Cut ribbon to desired length. Wrap around raw edge to conceal. Tie on teething ring as a bow.

How To

Baby Diaper Wrap

Use this when you are offering a casserole or baking gift to a new or expectant parent and they'll have a receiving blanket too.

Materials: Receiving blanket, cake or squares in 8 × 8 inch (20 × 20 cm) or 9 × 9 inch (22 × 22 cm) pan, cardboard cut to match size of pan top, tape, diaper pins, scissors, ribbon, soother.

1. If receiving blanket is rectangular, fold up 1 side to form square. Fold in each corner to center to form diamond. Points should be square.

2. Tape cardboard to top of pan to keep blanket clean and protect food if pan does not have lid of its own. Place pan in center of diamond with edges parallel to points. Fold point up over pan. Snug fabric to side of pan and fold over about 2 inches (5 cm), then fold point in to center. Repeat on opposite side.

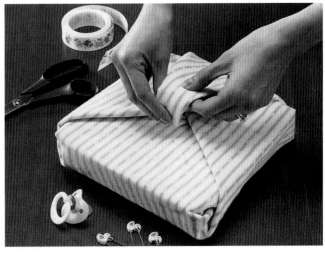

3. Fold up bottom. Tuck end underneath sides. Pin on both sides with diaper pin.

4. Cut ribbon to desired length. Attach soother with ribbon.

Carrot Cake

The marzipan carrots add a special touch to this classic cake.

Granulated sugar	1 3/4 cups	425 mL
Large eggs	4	4
Cooking oil	1 cup	250 mL
Grated carrot, lightly packed	2 cups	500 mL
Finely chopped pecans	1 cup	250 mL
All-purpose flour	2 cups	500 mL
Baking powder	2 tsp.	10 mL
Baking soda	1 tsp.	5 mL
Ground cinnamon	2 tsp.	10 mL
Salt	3/4 tsp.	4 mL
ICING		
Cream cheese, softened	2 oz.	62 g
Icing (confectioner's) sugar	2 cups	500 mL
Vanilla	1 tsp.	5 mL
Milk	3 tbsp.	50 mL
MARZIPAN CARROTS		
Marzipan (available at some bakeries or kitchen specialty stores)	1/4 cup	60 mL
Drops of yellow food coloring	3	3
Drops of red food coloring	1/2	1/2

Beat sugar and eggs together well in large bowl. Mix in cooking oil, carrot and pecans.

Stir next 5 ingredients in medium bowl. Add to egg mixture. Stir until just moistened. Turn into greased 12 cup (2.7 L) bundt pan. Bake in 350°F (175°C) oven for about 1 hour. Wooden pick inserted in center should come out clean. Let stand for 15 minutes before turning out onto wire rack to cool.

Icing: Beat first 3 ingredients together, adding enough milk to make a barely pourable glaze. Spoon over top of cake, allowing icing to run down sides. Cuts into 15 to 20 pieces.

1 piece (without Marzipan Carrots): 461 Calories; 24 g Total Fat; 292 mg Sodium; 5 g Protein; 59 g Carbohydrate; 2 g Dietary Fiber

Marzipan Carrots: Knead marzipan until pliable. Knead yellow food coloring and red food coloring into 3/4 of marzipan to make desired "carrot" shade of orange. Shape into about 6 carrots. Make shallow indents crosswise on carrots with tip of knife. Knead green food coloring into remaining marzipan. Shape into carrot tops and attach to carrots. Arrange "carrots" on top of icing.

Pictured below and on page 87.

Carrot Cake, this page

Mud Cake, below

Mud Cake

This cake is dark, rich and moist. The thick, creamy icing sets well and can be covered with plastic wrap for gift-giving.

All-purpose flour	2 1/4 cups	550 mL
Granulated sugar	2 cups	500 mL
Cocoa	1/2 cup	125 mL
Baking soda	1 tsp.	5 mL
Salt	3/4 tsp.	4 mL
Large eggs	2	2
Sour cream	3/4 cup	175 mL
Cooking oil	1/2 cup	125 mL
Vanilla	1 1/2 tsp.	7 mL
Boiling water	1 cup	250 mL

CHOCOLATE ICING

Icing (confectioner's) sugar	2 cups	500 mL
Cocoa	1/3 cup	75 mL
Vanilla	1/2 tsp.	2 mL
Hard margarine (or butter), softened	3 tbsp.	50 mL
Strong prepared coffee (or water)	3 tbsp.	50 mL

Gummie worms, for garnish

Combine first 10 ingredients in large bowl. Beat on low until moistened. Beat on medium for about 2 minutes until smooth. Batter will be thin. Turn into greased 9 x 13 inch (22 x 33 cm) pan. Bake in 350°F (175°C) oven for about 35 minutes. Wooden pick inserted in center should come out clean. Cool.

Chocolate Icing: Beat all 5 ingredients together in medium bowl. Add more icing sugar or coffee to make soft spreading consistency. Spread over cake. Makes 1 1/4 cups (300 mL) icing.

Add gummie worms on top for garnish. Cuts into 24 pieces.

1 piece: 236 Calories; 8.3 g Total Fat; 154 mg Sodium; 3 g Protein; 40 g Carbohydrate; 1 g Dietary Fiber

Pictured above.

Chocolate Orange Cake, page 97

Caramel Apple Cheesecake, this page

Caramel Apple Cheesecake

*A solid cheesecake with a thin layer of sliced apple
and caramel between crust and cheesecake.*

CRUST
Hard margarine (or butter), melted	1/2 cup	125 mL
Vanilla wafer crumbs	2 cups	500 mL

FILLING
Hard margarine (or butter), melted	2 tbsp.	30 mL
Granulated sugar	1 tsp.	5 mL
Sliced cooking apples (such as MacIntosh), about 2 medium	2 cups	500 mL
Caramel (or butterscotch) sundae topping	1/2 cup	125 mL
Light cream cheese, softened	16 oz.	500 g
Granulated sugar	1/2 cup	125 mL
Vanilla	1 tsp.	5 mL
Large eggs	2	2

TOPPINGS
Caramel (or butterscotch) sundae topping	1/2 cup	125 mL
Sliced almonds, toasted (see Note)	1/4 cup	60 mL

Crust: Melt margarine in medium saucepan. Stir in wafer crumbs. Press into bottom and 1 inch (2.5 cm) up sides of ungreased 9 inch (22 cm) springform pan. Bake in 350°F (175°C) oven for 10 minutes.

Filling: Combine margarine and first amount of sugar in frying pan. Add apple. Sauté until apple is soft but not mushy. Spoon over crust.

Drizzle first amount of sundae topping over apples. Cool.

Beat cream cheese, second amount of sugar and vanilla together in medium bowl. Beat in eggs, 1 at a time, until just blended. Pour over apple. Bake in 350°F (175°C) oven for 45 to 50 minutes until set. Cool completely. Chill. Cut or mark off into 12 wedges.

Topping: Spoon about 2 tsp. (10 mL) sundae topping over individual wedges. Sprinkle each with 1 tsp. (5 mL) almonds. Serves 12.

1 serving: 391 Calories; 22.4 g Total Fat; 563 mg Sodium; 7 g Protein; 44 g Carbohydrate; 1 g Dietary Fiber

Pictured above.

Note: To toast almonds, place in single layer in ungreased shallow pan. Bake in 350°F (175°C) oven for 5 to 10 minutes, stirring or shaking often, until desired doneness.

Chocolate Orange Cake

Milk chocolate flavor with delicate orange undertones. Use fruit roll ups to "tie" cake in ribbon.

Hard margarine (or butter), softened	1/2 cup	125 mL
Granulated sugar	3/4 cup	175 mL
Large eggs	2	2
Orange flavoring	2 tsp.	10 mL
Semisweet chocolate baking squares (1 oz., 28 g, each), cut up	3	3
Sour milk (1 tbsp., 15 mL, white vinegar plus milk)	3/4 cup	175 mL
All-purpose flour	2 cups	500 mL
Baking soda	1 tsp.	5 mL
Salt	1/2 tsp.	2 mL
ICING		
Light cream cheese, softened	8 oz.	250 g
Icing (confectioner's) sugar	4 cups	1 L
Cocoa, sifted if lumpy	1/2 cup	125 mL
Hard margarine (or butter), softened	1/4 cup	60 mL
Orange flavoring	2 tsp.	10 mL

Cream margarine and sugar together in large bowl. Beat in eggs, 1 at a time. Add orange flavoring. Beat.

Heat chocolate and sour milk in medium saucepan on medium-low, stirring often, until chocolate is melted. Mixture will look curdled. Cool until lukewarm.

Combine flour, baking soda and salt in medium bowl. Add to margarine mixture in 3 parts, alternately with chocolate mixture in 2 parts, beginning and ending with flour mixture. Divide between 2 greased and floured 8 inch (20 cm) round layer pans. Bake in 350°F (175°C) oven for about 25 minutes. Wooden pick inserted in center should come out clean. Cool.

Icing: Stir all 5 ingredients in medium bowl. Beat on low until mixed. Beat on medium until smooth and creamy. Fill and frost cake. Cuts into 12 wedges.

1 wedge: 512 Calories; 20 g Total Fat; 513 mg Sodium; 7 g Protein; 80 g Carbohydrate; 2 g Dietary Fiber

Pictured on page 96.

Pumpkin Chocolate Mini-Cheesecakes

Little pumpkin treats for your Thanksgiving dinner host or for the next Halloween party.

FIRST LAYER		
Gingersnap cookies (2 inch, 5 cm, size)	24	24
FILLING		
Light cream cheese, softened	16 oz.	500 g
Granulated sugar	2/3 cup	150 mL
Large eggs	2	2
Can of pumpkin (without spice)	14 oz.	398 mL
Light sour cream	1 cup	250 mL
All-purpose flour	2 tbsp.	30 mL
Ground cinnamon	3/4 tsp.	4 mL
Ground nutmeg	1/2 tsp.	2 mL
Ground ginger	1/2 tsp.	2 mL
Salt	1/2 tsp.	2 mL
Semisweet chocolate chips, melted	1/2 cup	125 mL

First layer: Put 1 gingersnap, flat side down, into each of 24 muffin paper liners in muffin cups.

Filling: Beat cream cheese and sugar together in large bowl until smooth. Beat in eggs, 1 at a time, beating only until blended. Add pumpkin, sour cream, flour, cinnamon, nutmeg, ginger and salt. Mix. Measure and set aside 1/4 cup (60 mL) batter. Pour 1/4 cup (60 mL) remaining batter over each gingersnap.

Stir melted chocolate into reserved batter. Drop by teaspoonfuls on top of batter in muffin cups. Using tip of knife, marble into batter slightly. Bake in 350°F (175°C) oven for 30 to 35 minutes until set. Wooden pick inserted in center should come out clean. Makes 24 mini-cheesecakes.

1 mini-cheesecake: 140 Calories; 7 g Total Fat; 251 mg Sodium; 4 g Protein; 17 g Carbohydrate; 1 g Dietary Fiber

Pictured below.

Fudge Sauce

A rich thick and glossy sauce that's not too sweet.
Any home would love a small jar as a gift.

Unsweetened baking chocolate squares (1 oz., 28 g, each), cut up	6	6
Can of skim evaporated milk	13 1/2 oz.	385 mL
Milk	1/4 cup	60 mL
Granulated sugar	1 cup	250 mL
Corn syrup	1 1/2 tbsp.	25 mL
Instant coffee granules (optional)	1/2 – 1 tsp.	2 – 5 mL
Salt	1/4 tsp.	1 mL

Combine all 7 ingredients in large saucepan. Heat and stir on medium until boiling. Boil for about 2 minutes. Cool. Pour into small jars. Makes 2 1/2 cups (625 mL).

1/4 cup (60 mL): 206 Calories; 9.1 g Total Fat; 115 mg Sodium; 5 g Protein; 32 g Carbohydrate; 3 g Dietary Fiber

Pictured on page 99.

DIRECTIONS FOR

Fudge Sauce, Pineapple Sauce and Strawberry Orange Sauce:
Serve over ice cream or pound cake. Keep chilled. Keeps for at least 1 month.

Pineapple Sauce

Thick sauce with bits of pineapple throughout.
Pineapple lovers will appreciate the fruity flavor.

Can of crushed pineapple, with juice	14 oz.	398 mL
Granulated sugar	1/4 cup	60 mL
Water	2 tbsp.	30 mL
Cornstarch	1 tbsp.	15 mL

Heat pineapple with juice and sugar in small saucepan, stirring often, until boiling.

Stir water into cornstarch in small cup until smooth. Gradually stir into pineapple mixture. Heat and stir until boiling and thickened. Cool. Pour into small jars. Makes 1 3/4 cups (425 mL).

1/4 cup (60 mL): 67 Calories; trace Total Fat; 1 mg Sodium; trace Protein; 17 g Carbohydrate; 1 g Dietary Fiber

Pictured on page 99.

Strawberry Orange Sauce

Beautiful, dark red color with lots of chunky bits of strawberry.
Great strawberry flavor!

Fresh (or frozen, thawed) strawberries, mashed	3 cups	750 mL
Brown sugar, packed	1/4 cup	60 mL
Cornstarch	2 tbsp.	30 mL
Orange marmalade	2 tbsp.	30 mL
Orange liqueur (optional)	1 tbsp.	15 mL

Place strawberries in saucepan. Add brown sugar, cornstarch, marmalade and liqueur. Stir. Heat and stir on medium until thickened slightly. Cool. Pour into small jars. Makes 2 1/3 cups (575 mL).

1/4 cup (60 mL): 54 Calories; trace Total Fat; 5 mg Sodium; trace Protein; 14 g Carbohydrate; 1 g Dietary Fiber

Pictured on page 99.

Open jars, in clockwise direction:

Right: Strawberry Orange Sauce, above
Bottom: Fudge Sauce, this page
Upper Left: Pineapple Sauce, above

Top: Strawberry Rhubarb Streusel Pie, below
Bottom: Apple Cranberry Pie, this page

Strawberry Rhubarb Streusel Pie

This pie offers a nice blend of sweet and tart, and cuts nicely after baking.

Chopped fresh (or frozen, thawed) rhubarb	3 cups	750 mL
Sliced fresh (or frozen, thawed) strawberries	1 cup	250 mL
Granulated sugar	1 cup	250 mL
All-purpose flour	3 tbsp.	50 mL
Lemon juice	1/2 tsp.	2 mL
Unbaked 9 inch (22 cm) pie shell	1	1
TOPPING		
All-purpose flour	2/3 cup	150 mL
Brown sugar, packed	1/2 cup	125 mL
Ground cinnamon	1/2 tsp.	2 mL
Hard margarine (or butter)	1/3 cup	75 mL

Combine rhubarb, strawberries, sugar, flour and lemon juice in large bowl. Stir until combined. Turn into pie shell.

Topping: Combine flour, brown sugar and cinnamon in large bowl. Cut in margarine until crumbly. Sprinkle over rhubarb mixture. Bake in 375°F (190°C) oven for about 50 minutes. Cuts into 8 wedges.

1 wedge: 383 Calories; 13.4 g Total Fat; 204 mg Sodium; 3 g Protein; 65 g Carbohydrate; 2 g Dietary Fiber

Pictured above.

Apple Cranberry Pie

A bright red filling peeks through the lattice top beautifully.

Pastry for a 2 crust (9 inch, 22 cm) pie, your own or a mix	1	1
Fresh (or frozen, thawed) cranberries	2 1/2 cups	625 mL
Granulated sugar	1 3/4 cups	425 mL
Minute tapioca	1/3 cup	75 mL
Water	1/4 cup	60 mL
Grated lemon peel (optional)	1 tsp.	5 mL
Peeled, cored and sliced tart cooking apples (such as Granny Smith)	2 1/2 cups	625 mL

Roll out pastry. Line bottom of pie plate. Roll out top crust.

Combine next 5 ingredients in large saucepan. Bring to a boil. Remove from heat.

Stir in apples. Let cool for about 20 minutes, stirring occasionally. Turn into pie shell. Make a lattice top with remaining pastry. Press to seal. Trim. Bake in 350°F (175°C) oven for about 55 minutes until tender. Cuts into 8 wedges.

1 wedge: 400 Calories; 10.6 g Total Fat; 205 mg Sodium; 2 g Protein; 77 g Carbohydrate; 2 g Dietary Fiber

Pictured on this page.

Dinners

When friends or family are faced with stressful times, offering a meal, packaged and ready to cook or reheat when needed, is always a welcome gift. A roast, stroganoff, quiche or casserole takes the cooking burden off a spouse whose partner is ill, or a home faced with unexpected company.

Be sure your dish is clearly marked on the covering with any cooking instructions and the date it was made, in case they decide to freeze it. You may also want to add your name (and phone number if necessary) to the bottom of the dish.

Stew Stroganoff, page 112

Oven Pot Roast

*Take this delicious pot roast to a friend right in
the roaster or slice and add to gravy and
vegetables in a disposable foil pan.*

Boneless blade (or chuck) roast	3 lbs.	1.4 kg
Medium potatoes, quartered	4	4
Pearl onions, peeled (about 40)	1/2 lb.	225 g
Baby carrots	1/2 lb.	225 g
Sliced celery	1 cup	250 mL
Can of condensed tomato soup	10 oz.	284 mL
Prepared orange juice	1/2 cup	125 mL
Red wine vinegar	1/2 cup	125 mL
Salt	1 tsp.	5 mL
Pepper	1/2 tsp.	2 mL
Bay leaf	1	1

Set roast in center of medium roaster. Surround with potato,
onions, carrots and celery.

Stir soup vigorously in medium bowl. Add orange juice,
vinegar, salt and pepper. Mix. Add bay leaf. Pour over roast
and vegetables making sure bay leaf is in liquid. Cover. Bake
in 300°F (150°C) oven for 3 to 3 1/2 hours until roast
and vegetables are tender. Remove and discard bay leaf.
Serves 8.

*1 serving: 423 Calories; 19.3 g Total Fat; 687 mg Sodium; 39 g Protein;
23 g Carbohydrate; 2 g Dietary Fiber*

Pictured on page 102 and page 103.

Photo Legend previous page:

Top Left: Oven Pot Roast, above
Centre Right: Quiche Lorraine, page 105
Bottom: Pork And Bean Stroganoff, this page

Pork And Bean Stroganoff

*This dish includes beans in a tomato sauce,
an unusual but tasty addition. Include a package of broad
noodles in your gift and the meal is complete.*

Medium onion, chopped	1	1
Hard margarine (or butter)	1 tbsp.	15 mL
Cooking oil	1 tbsp.	15 mL
All-purpose flour	1/4 cup	60 mL
Pork tenderloin, cut into thin strips	1 lb.	454 g
Cooking oil	1 tbsp.	15 mL
Salt, sprinkle		
Pepper, sprinkle		
Water	3/4 cup	175 mL
Chicken bouillon powder	1 tsp.	5 mL
Whole small fresh mushrooms	1 cup	250 mL
Can of beans in tomato sauce	14 oz.	398 mL
Parsley flakes	2 tsp.	10 mL
Light sour cream	1/2 cup	125 mL

Sauté onion in margarine and first amount of cooking oil in
non-stick frying pan until soft. Remove to plate. Set aside.

Measure flour into medium bowl or resealable plastic bag.
Dredge pork in flour until well coated. Add to frying pan
with second amount of cooking oil. Sprinkle with salt and
pepper. Sear until lightly browned.

Add water, bouillon powder, mushrooms and onion
mixture. Heat and stir until boiling. Reduce heat. Cover.
Simmer for about 10 minutes until pork is tender.

Add beans, parsley and sour cream. Stir to heat through.
Makes 5 cups (1.25 L). Serves 4.

*1 serving: 403 Calories; 15.6 g Total Fat; 693 mg Sodium; 35 g Protein;
33 g Carbohydrate; 9 g Dietary Fiber*

Pictured on page 102/103.

*DIRECTIONS FOR
Pork And Bean Stroganoff: Heat in large saucepan, stirring
often. Do not boil. Serve over broad noodles.*

Quiche Lorraine

We owe thanks to the Alsace region of France for this.
The removable bottom of the flan pan
makes a very attractive edge.

PASTRY

All-purpose flour	1 1/2 cups	375 mL
Salt	1/4 tsp.	1 mL
Hard margarine (or butter)	6 tbsp.	100 mL
Water	1/4 cup	60 mL

FILLING

Bacon slices, diced	8	8
Chopped onion	1/2 cup	125 mL
Large eggs	4	4
Milk	1 1/2 cups	375 mL
Salt	1/4 tsp.	1 mL
Grated Gruyère cheese	1 cup	250 mL
Pepper	1/8 tsp.	0.5 mL
Ground nutmeg, just a pinch		

Pastry: Combine flour and salt in large bowl. Cut in margarine until consistency of fine bread crumbs.

Sprinkle with enough water to form a soft ball. Roll out pastry to line 8 inch (20 cm) flan pan.

Filling: Sauté bacon and onion in frying pan for about 7 minutes until onion is soft and bacon is cooked. Drain well. Cool thoroughly. Scatter over bottom of pastry shell.

Beat eggs in medium bowl until frothy.

Add remaining 5 ingredients. Mix. Pour over bacon mixture. Bake on bottom rack in 350°F (175°C) oven for about 60 minutes until firm and lightly browned. Cuts into 6 wedges.

1 wedge: 433 Calories; 26.3 g Total Fat; 607 mg Sodium; 18 g Protein; 30 g Carbohydrate; 1 g Dietary Fiber

Pictured on page 103.

Variation: A 9 inch (22 cm) pie plate may be used instead of a flan pan.

Shepherd's Pie

A cloud of creamy potatoes nestled on a bed
of ground beef and colorful vegetables.

Potatoes (about 9 medium), cut up	4 lbs.	1.8 kg
Boiling water		
Lean ground beef	3 lbs.	1.4 kg
Chopped onion (about 2 large)	2 cups	500 mL
Cooking oil	1 tbsp.	15 mL
All-purpose flour	1/4 cup	60 mL
Seasoned salt	1 tsp.	5 mL
Salt	3/4 tsp.	4 mL
Pepper	1/2 tsp.	2 mL
Water	1 cup	250 mL
Liquid gravy browner	2 tsp.	10 mL
Prepared horseradish	2 tsp.	10 mL
Chopped tomato (about 2 medium)	1 1/4 cups	300 mL
Diced carrot, cooked	2 cups	500 mL
Frozen peas, cooked	2 cups	500 mL
Diced celery, cooked	1/2 cup	125 mL
Steak sauce (such as HP)	2 tbsp.	30 mL
Hard margarine (or butter)	6 tbsp.	100 mL
Milk	1 cup	250 mL
Salt	1/2 tsp.	2 mL
Pepper	1/4 tsp.	1 mL

Paprika, sprinkle

Cook potato in boiling water in large saucepan or Dutch oven for about 20 minutes until tender. Drain. Mash. Set aside.

Scramble-fry ground beef and onion, in 2 batches, in cooking oil in frying pan for about 8 minutes. Drain.

Sprinkle with flour, seasoned salt, salt and pepper. Mix well. Add water. Heat and stir until boiling and thickened.

Add next 7 ingredients. Stir. Divide mixture between 2 greased 8 x 8 inch (20 x 20 cm) pans.

Add margarine, milk, salt and pepper to potato. Mash well. Divide between both pans, gently spreading over meat mixture. Spray potato well with cooking spray.

Sprinkle with paprika. Bake, uncovered, in top 1/3 of 350°F (175°C) oven for about 30 minutes until heated through and lightly browned. Each pan serves 6, for a total of 12 servings.

1 serving: 391 Calories; 17 g Total Fat; 510 mg Sodium; 25 g Protein; 34 g Carbohydrate; 4 g Dietary Fiber

Pictured on page 106.

How To

Tea Towel Cozy

You can dress up a metal or foil pan with tea towels for someone to keep. It also works to keep hot food warm during transportation.

Materials: 2 tea towels, casserole, cake or squares in 8 x 8 inch (20 x 20 cm) or 9 x 9 inch (22 x 22 cm) pan, cardboard cut to match size of pan top, scissors, ribbon.

1. Fold in sides of 1 tea towel to width of pan. Place second tea towel at right angles over first. Fold in sides to width of pan.

2. Place pan in center. Fold up sides of top tea towel, overlapping one another. Repeat with second tea towel. Fold under ends of last side if desired.

3. Cut ribbon to desired length. Tie ribbon around pan to secure tea towels.

Shepherd's Pie, page 105.

Taco Pie

Everyone will love this dinner! Send it along with shredded lettuce, chopped tomato, salsa and sour cream garnishes. Absolutely wonderful.

Lean ground beef	1 lb.	454 g
Chopped onion	1 cup	250 mL
Can of tomato sauce	7 1/2 oz.	213 mL
Envelope of taco seasoning	1 1/4 oz.	35 g
Package of refrigerator crescent-style rolls (8 rolls per tube)	8 1/2 oz.	235 g
Crushed corn chips	1 cup	250 mL
Sour cream	1 cup	250 mL
Grated medium Cheddar cheese	1/2 cup	125 mL
Grated part-skim mozzarella cheese	1/2 cup	125 mL
Crushed corn chips	1/3 cup	75 mL

Scramble-fry ground beef and onion in frying pan until beef is no longer pink. Drain.

Add tomato sauce and taco seasoning. Stir well.

Press crescent rolls together to form crust in ungreased 9 inch (22 cm) pie plate. Sprinkle with first amount of corn chips. Spoon beef mixture over top.

Drop dabs of sour cream here and there over beef mixture. Spread as best you can. Sprinkle with cheddar and mozzarella cheese. Scatter second amount of corn chips over cheese. Bake in 375°F (190°C) oven for about 25 minutes until hot and crust is browned. Cuts into 6 wedges.

1 wedge: 361 Calories; 21.2 g Total Fat; 1251 mg Sodium; 22 g Protein; 21 g Carbohydrate; 2 g Dietary Fiber

Pictured on page 113.

DIRECTIONS FOR
Taco Pie: Reheat chilled pie in 325°F (160°C) oven for 30 to 40 minutes until hot. Let stand for 10 minutes. Sprinkle with shredded lettuce and chopped tomato. Cut into 6 wedges. Garnish individual servings with salsa and sour cream.

Tuna Pineapple Casserole

A traditional standby with a flavor twist of pineapple and curry.

Can of condensed cream of mushroom soup	10 oz.	284 mL
Can of pineapple tidbits, drained and juice reserved	14 oz.	398 mL
Can of sliced mushrooms, drained	10 oz.	284 mL
Chopped almonds	1/4 cup	60 mL
Salt	1 tsp.	5 mL
Curry powder	1 tsp.	5 mL
Reserved pineapple juice	1/4 cup	60 mL
Cooked long grain white rice	1 1/4 cups	300 mL
Cans of flaked tuna, drained (6 1/2 oz., 184 g, each)	2	2
Hard margarine (or butter)	1 tbsp.	15 mL
Dry bread crumbs	1/4 cup	60 mL

Combine soup, pineapple, mushrooms, almonds, salt and curry powder in large saucepan. Stir well. Heat, stirring often. Add pineapple juice and rice. Stir.

Add tuna. Stir gently. Turn into greased 2 quart (2 L) casserole.

Melt margarine in small saucepan. Add bread crumbs. Stir. Sprinkle on top of casserole. Cover. Bake in 350°F (175°C) oven for about 30 minutes until hot. Makes 5 1/2 cups (1.4 L). Serves 4.

1 serving: 396 Calories; 14.5 g Total Fat; 1626 mg Sodium; 18 g Protein; 50 g Carbohydrate; 4 g Dietary Fiber

Pictured below.

Salmon Pie

This makes a fabulous substantial dinner.
Send sauce in container with tight-fitting lid.

Medium potatoes, quartered	5	5
Boiling water		
Chopped onion	1 cup	250 mL
Hard margarine (or butter)	2 tbsp.	30 mL
Onion salt	1/2 tsp.	2 mL
Salt	1/2 tsp.	2 mL
Pepper	1/4 tsp.	1 mL
Fresh dill (or 1/2 tsp., 2 mL, dried)	2 tsp.	10 mL
Milk	2 tbsp.	30 mL
Cans of red salmon (7.5 oz., 213 g, each), drained, 1/3 cup (75 mL) liquid reserved, skin and round bones removed, flaked	2	2
Pastry for 2 crust 9 inch (22 cm) pie, your own or a mix		
SAUCE		
Hard margarine (or butter), melted	1/4 cup	60 mL
All-purpose flour	1/4 cup	60 mL
Salt	1/8 tsp.	0.5 mL
Pepper	1/8 tsp.	0.5 mL
Paprika	1/4 tsp.	1 mL
Milk	1 2/3 cups	400 mL
Reserved salmon liquid	1/3 cup	75 mL

Fresh dill, for garnish

Cook potatoes in boiling water until tender. Drain. Mash. Set aside.

Sauté onion in margarine in small frying pan until onion is soft. Add to potatoes. Stir.

Add next 4 ingredients to potato mixture. Mash. Potato mixture should be stiff. Add milk. Mash.

Add salmon. Stir. Cool to lukewarm.

Roll out 2/3 of pastry and fit into 9 inch (22 cm) pie plate. Trim. Spoon potato mixture into pie shell. Roll out top crust. Dampen outside edge of pastry with water. Fit on top crust. Trim and crimp to seal. Cut slits in top. Bake in 400°F (205°C) oven for about 35 minutes until browned.

Sauce: Combine margarine, flour, salt, pepper and paprika in saucepan. Add milk and reserved salmon liquid. Heat and stir until boiling and thickened. Pour into serving bowl. Makes about 2 cups (500 mL) sauce. Serve on the side.

Sprinkle individual servings with dill. Serves 6.

1 serving: 553 Calories; 31.1 g Total Fat; 981 mg Sodium; 14 g Protein; 54 g Carbohydrate; 2 Dietary Fiber

Pictured on page 113.

Stew Stroganoff

Here's a stew that delivers wonderful beefy flavor and a zesty stroganoff base.

Boneless inside round (or blade or chuck) steak, trimmed of fat and cut bite size	2 lbs.	900 g
Cooking oil	1 tbsp.	15 mL
Water, to cover		
Beef bouillon powder	2 tbsp.	30 mL
Salt	1/2 tsp.	2 mL
Pepper	1/2 tsp.	2 mL
Cubed potatoes	4 cups	1 L
Diced carrot	3 cups	750 mL
Cubed yellow turnip	1 cup	250 mL
Coarsely chopped onion	2 cups	500 mL
Water	1/4 cup	60 mL
All-purpose flour	2 tbsp.	30 mL
Light sour cream	1 cup	250 mL

Sear beef in cooking oil in large uncovered pot or Dutch oven for about 5 minutes.

Add water, bouillon powder, salt and pepper. Bring to a boil. Reduce heat. Cover. Simmer for 1 3/4 hours until beef is very tender.

Add potato, carrot, turnip and onion. Stir. Cover. Simmer for 25 minutes until vegetables are tender.

Stir water into flour in small cup until smooth. Gradually stir into simmering liquid. Heat and stir until thickened.

Stir in sour cream. Heat and stir until heated through. Do not boil. Makes 10 cups (2.5 L) stew. Serves 8.

1 serving: 293 Calories; 6.8 g Total Fat; 718 mg Sodium; 31 g Protein; 27 g Carbohydrate; 3 g Dietary Fiber

Pictured on page 113 and on page 101.

Top and Bottom: Salmon Pie, this page
Center Left: Stew Stroganoff, above
Center Right: Taco Pie, page 111

Healing Chicken Soup

*Make this comforting soup for your dear friend
when she's down with a bad cold!*

Boneless, skinless chicken breast half, diced	4 oz.	113 g
Chopped onion	1/2 cup	125 mL
Thinly sliced celery	1/2 cup	125 mL
Diced carrot	2/3 cup	150 mL
Olive (or cooking) oil	1 tbsp.	15 mL
Cans of condensed chicken broth (10 oz., 284 mL, each)	2	2
Water	3 cups	750 mL
Parsley flakes	2 tsp.	10 mL
Bay leaf	1	1
Uncooked medium egg noodles	2 cups	500 mL
Boiling water	4 cups	1 L
Salt	1 tsp.	5 mL

Sauté chicken, onion, celery and carrot in olive oil in large saucepan for 10 minutes until onion is golden and chicken is no longer pink.

Add chicken broth, water, parsley and bay leaf. Simmer, covered, for 30 minutes until carrots are soft. Remove and discard bay leaf. Cool. Makes 6 2/3 cups (1.65 L) broth mixture.

Cook noodles in boiling water and salt in large saucepan for 7 to 9 minutes until tender but firm. Drain. Rinse well under cold water. Drain. Divide noodles between two 1 quart (4 cup, 1 L) jars. Fill with cooled broth mixture. Makes about 8 cups (2 L).

1 cup (250 mL): 102 Calories; 3.2 g Total Fat; 488 mg Sodium; 8 g Protein; 10 g Carbohydrate; 1 g Dietary Fiber

Pictured on this page.

Tropical Chicken And Rice

*This casserole has a pretty presentation.
Very tropical with the pineapple, ginger and coconut.*

Finely chopped onion	3/4 cup	175 mL
Medium red pepper, chopped	1	1
Apple cider vinegar	1/2 cup	125 mL
Reserved pineapple juice, plus water to make	2 cups	500 mL
Brown sugar, packed	3 tbsp.	50 mL
Soy sauce	1 1/2 tbsp.	25 mL
Ground ginger	1/2 tsp.	2 mL
Salt	1/2 tsp.	2 mL
Water	1/2 cup	125 mL
Cornstarch	2 1/2 tbsp.	37 mL
Chopped cooked chicken	3 cups	750 mL
Cooked long grain white rice	4 cups	1 L
Coconut	1/3 cup	75 mL
Can of pineapple rings, drained and juice reserved	19 oz.	540 mL
Green pepper, sliced into rings	1	1
Paprika, sprinkle		

Combine first 8 ingredients in medium saucepan. Bring to a boil.

Stir water into cornstarch in small cup until smooth. Gradually stir into onion mixture. Heat and stir until boiling and thickened. Reduce heat. Simmer, uncovered, for about 5 minutes.

Add chicken. Stir. Pour chicken mixture into ungreased 3 quart (3 L) casserole. Spread rice over top. Sprinkle with coconut.

Layer pineapple and green pepper rings over coconut. Sprinkle with paprika. Cover. Bake in 350°F (175°C) oven for about 45 minutes. Serves 6.

1 serving: 473 Calories; 7.4 g Total Fat; 555 mg Sodium; 29 g Protein; 73 g Carbohydrate; 3 g Dietary Fiber

Pictured below.

Top: Tropical Chicken And Rice, this page
Bottom: Healing Chicken Soup, this page

Dry Mixes

Perfect gifts for delivering near or far, these dry mixes need little or no additional ingredients to transform them into scrumptious edibles. Wrap up some seasoning mixes for a fledgling cook to spice up his or her kitchen efforts. Know someone in university surviving on macaroni and cheese? They'll appreciate a medley of rice mixes or a hearty soup mix to help them get by. Give a movie rental gift certificate with a jar of flavored popcorn seasoning to a couch potato.

Cappuccino Mix, page 128

Basic Seasoning

Italian Seasoning

Layered Cran-Raisin on Cookies — directions back

Garam Masala

Cajun Spice

Recipe for:
from the kitchen

Basic Seasoning

A great substitute for salt and therefore great with just about everything.

Paprika	1/4 cup	60 mL
Poultry seasoning	2 tsp.	10 mL
Garlic powder	2 tsp.	10 mL
Celery seed	2 tsp.	10 mL
Onion powder	1 1/2 tsp.	7 mL
Curry powder	1 tsp.	5 mL

Combine all 6 ingredients in small bowl. Spoon into small jar with tight-fitting lid. Makes about 6 tbsp. (100 mL).

1 tsp. (5 mL): 8 Calories; 0.3 g Total Fat; 1 mg Sodium; trace Protein; 2 g Carbohydrate; trace Dietary Fiber

Pictured on page 116.

Cajun Spice

For when you want to spice things up a bit.

Salt	2 tbsp.	30 mL
Pepper	1 tsp.	5 mL
Garlic powder	1 tsp.	5 mL
Chili powder	1 tsp.	5 mL
Cayenne pepper	2 tsp.	10 mL
Dried whole oregano, crushed	1/2 tsp.	2 mL
Dried thyme	1/2 tsp.	2 mL
Onion powder	1 tsp.	5 mL

Combine all 8 ingredients in small bowl. Spoon into small jar with tight-fitting lid. Makes about 1/4 cup (60 mL).

1 tsp. (5 mL): 1 Calorie; 0 g Total Fat; 393 mg Sodium; trace Protein; trace Carbohydrate; trace Dietary Fiber

Pictured on page 116.

Photo Legend previous page:

1. Basic Seasoning, above
2. Italian Seasoning, this page
3. Cran Raisin Cookie Mix, page 119
4. Sugar Cookie Mix, page 119
5. Cakey Brownie Mix, page 119
6. Sugar Cookies, page 119, with Easy Icing, page 120
7. Cajun Spice, above
8. Garam Masala, this page

Italian Seasoning

A welcome addition to a pasta dish, salad or even meatloaf.

Ground savory	1 tbsp.	15 mL
Dried rosemary	1 tbsp.	15 mL
Dried thyme	1 tbsp.	15 mL
Dried whole oregano	1 tbsp.	15 mL
Dried sweet basil	1 tbsp.	15 mL
Ground sage	2 tsp.	10 mL
Dried whole marjoram	2 tsp.	10 mL
Dried crushed chilies (optional)	1 tsp.	5 mL

Combine all 8 ingredients in small bowl. Spoon into small jar with tight-fitting lid. Makes about 6 tbsp. (100 mL).

1 tsp. (5 mL): 4 Calories; 0.1 g Total Fat; trace Sodium; trace Protein; 1 g Carbohydrate; trace Dietary Fiber

Pictured on page 116.

Garam Masala

Gah-RAHM mah-SAH-lah is an Indian spice mix known for its warmth for body and soul.

Ground cinnamon	1 tbsp.	15 mL
Ground nutmeg	2 tsp.	10 mL
Ground cumin	1 tbsp.	15 mL
Ground cardamom	1 tbsp.	15 mL
Ground ginger	1 tbsp.	15 mL
Ground coriander	1 tbsp.	15 mL
Pepper	1 1/2 tsp.	7 mL
Ground cloves	1 tsp.	5 mL
Ground mace	1 1/2 tsp.	7 mL

Combine all 9 ingredients in small bowl. Spoon into small jar with tight-fitting lid. Makes about 1/2 cup (125 mL).

1 tsp. (5 mL): 6 Calories; 0.2 Total Fat; 1 mg Sodium; trace Protein; 1 g Carbohydrate; trace Dietary Fiber

Pictured on page 116.

DIRECTIONS FOR
Basic Seasoning, Cajun Spice, Italian Seasoning, Garam Masala: Use to season meat, fish or vegetables. Store in cool, dry place for up to 6 months.

Cran Raisin Cookie Mix

Not only a pretty gift to give but also a delicious cookie to eat!

All-purpose flour	3/4 cup	175 mL
Quick-cooking rolled oats (not instant)	1/2 cup	125 mL
All-purpose flour	3/4 cup	175 mL
Baking soda	1/2 tsp.	2 mL
Salt	1/2 tsp.	2 mL
Brown sugar, packed	1/3 cup	75 mL
Granulated sugar	1/3 cup	75 mL
Dried cranberries	1/4 cup	60 mL
Dark raisins	1/4 cup	60 mL
Candy-coated chocolate candy (such as M & M's)	1/2 cup	125 mL
Pecans (or walnuts), chopped	1/2 cup	125 mL

Layer all 11 ingredients, in order given, in large jar with tight-fitting lid. Makes about 4 cups (1 L).

Pictured on page 116.

DIRECTIONS FOR

Cran Raisin Cookies: Cream 3/4 cup (175 mL) softened hard margarine (or butter), 1 large egg and 1 tsp. (5 mL) vanilla together in medium bowl until fluffy. Add contents of jar. Mix by hand until well combined. Drop by heaping tablespoonfuls onto greased cookie sheet. Bake in 350°F (175°C) oven for about 16 minutes until edges start to brown. Cool on cookie sheet for 5 minutes. Remove cookies to wire rack to cool completely. Makes about 36 (3 dozen) cookies.

1 cookie: 110 Calories; 6.1 g Total Fat; 104 mg Sodium; 1 g Protein; 13 g Carbohydrate; 1 g Dietary Fiber

Cakey Brownie Mix

A fun-looking gift but an even better-tasting brownie.

Granulated sugar	1 1/4 cups	300 mL
Cocoa, sifted if lumpy	1/2 cup	125 mL
All-purpose flour	1 1/2 cups	375 mL
Baking powder	1 tsp.	5 mL
Baking soda	1/4 tsp.	1 mL
Salt	1/2 tsp.	2 mL
Chopped walnuts	1/2 cup	125 mL
White (or semisweet) chocolate chips	1/2 cup	125 mL

Layer all 8 ingredients, in order given, in large jar with tight-fitting lid. Makes about 4 cups (1 L).

Pictured on page 117.

DIRECTIONS FOR

Cakey Brownies: Empty contents of jar into large bowl. Add 1 tsp. (5 mL) vanilla, 2/3 cup (150 mL) cooking oil, 3 large eggs and 1/4 cup (60 mL) water. Mix for about 15 strokes. Turn into greased 8 x 8 inch (20 x 20 cm) pan. Bake in 350°F (175°C) oven for about 40 minutes. Wooden pick inserted in center should come out clean. Cool. Cuts into 16 pieces.

1 piece: 271 Calories; 15.1 g Total Fat; 135 mg Sodium; 4 g Protein; 32 g Carbohydrate; 1 g Dietary Fiber

Sugar Cookie Mix

A soft cookie that can be decorated using Easy Icing, page 120.

All-purpose flour	3 cups	750 mL
Baking powder	1 1/2 tsp.	7 mL
Salt	1 1/2 tsp.	7 mL
Granulated sugar	1 1/3 cups	325 mL
Vegetable shortening	3/4 cup	175 mL

Combine flour, baking powder, salt and sugar in large bowl. Cut in shortening until crumbly. Spoon into large resealable plastic bag or jar with tight-fitting lid. Makes 6 cups (1.5 L).

Pictured on page 116/117.

DIRECTIONS FOR

Sugar Cookies: Beat 1 large egg, 1/2 tsp. (2 mL) almond (or lemon) flavoring and 2 tbsp. (30 mL) milk (or cream) together in medium bowl. Add 2 cups (500 mL) Sugar Cookie Mix. Stir. Form into a ball. Turn out onto generously floured or sugared surface. Chill dough for easier rolling. Roll dough to 1/8 inch (3 mm) thickness. Cut with cookie cutters into desired shapes. Sprinkle with colored sugar. Bake on greased cookie sheet on center rack in 400°F (205°C) oven for about 7 minutes until edges start to brown. Remove cookies to wire rack to cool. Makes about 24 (2 dozen) cookies.

1 cookie: 170 Calories; 7.2 g Total Fat; 175 mg Sodium; 2 g Protein; 24 g Carbohydrate; 1 g Dietary Fiber

How To

Theme Gifts

When you let your imagination run wild, you can tailor a gift for someone special that he or she will love.

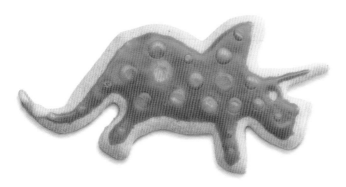

Think about their interests, jobs or hobbies. Head to a craft, toy, hardware or dollar store for trinkets and embellishments to go with your gift. For example, tie in a child's gift of miniature bakeware with dinosaurs. Find dinosaur wrapping paper, cookie cutters and miniature toys. This is a great idea for a birthday party too. The same gift could have a theme of dolls, trucks or bugs.

It doesn't matter whether you're preparing a gift for an adult or child; plenty of adult green thumbs would enjoy Mud Cake (shown on page 95) decorated with jelly worms and a miniature shovel, or Carrot Cake (shown on page 94) decorated with seeds and miniature garden tools. And regardless of age, a gift of Dark or Pink Popcorn Balls decorated with toy rats and skeletons will be appreciated at Halloween (shown on page 61).

If you're stuck for ideas, brainstorm with friends who enjoy doing crafts. You don't need special talents to think of a theme and carry it through.

Easy Icing

Water	2 tsp.	10 mL
Icing (confectioner's) sugar	1/2 cup	125 mL
Drops of food coloring	1 - 3	1 - 3

Stir water into icing sugar in small bowl until smooth. Add more water or icing sugar as needed to make barely pourable consistency.

Mix in food coloring, 1 drop at a time, until desired color is reached.

Paint icing on cookies with small paintbrush. For swirls, dip wooden pick into different colored icing. Make circular pattern in first layer of icing on cookie while still wet. Make polka dots by dabbing different color icing on first layer of wet icing.

Pictured on this page and on page 116/117.

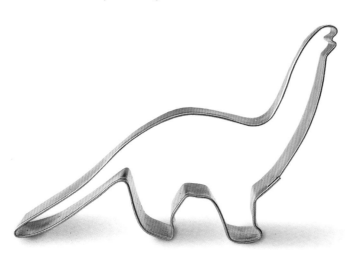

How To

Stamping Labels And Tags

Use paper, cardstock or adhesive labels to print a bunch of pretty gift tags to grab when you need! Or purchase self-adhesive labels from a stationery store to decorate.

Materials: Stamp pad, rubber stamps, paper, embossing powder, heat gun, markers, hole punch, pinking shears (or other design-edged scissors), ribbon.

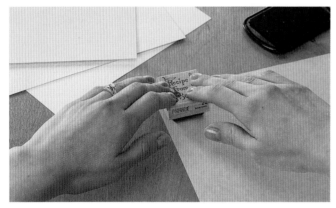

1. Apply ink to stamp. Press stamp to paper firmly and evenly.

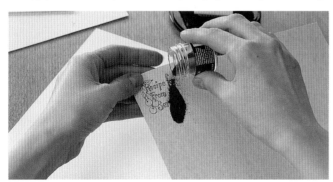

2. Sprinkle embossing powder generously over wet ink. Tap excess powder off onto scrap piece of paper. To reuse excess powder, fold scrap to form funnel and pour powder back into container.

3. Melt embossing powder with heat gun. It will appear shiny when melted and have a texture.

4. Color pattern with markers. Make hole with hole punch. Cut out tag with pinking shears. Thread ribbon through hole.

Spanish Rice Mix

This mix makes rice rich in flavor with an added bite from the chili powder.

Long grain white rice, uncooked	2 cups	500 mL
Parsley flakes	2 tsp.	10 mL
Dried whole oregano	1 tsp.	5 mL
Dried sweet basil	1 tsp.	5 mL
Beef bouillon powder	1 tsp.	5 mL
Minced onion flakes	2 tbsp.	30 mL
Granulated sugar	2 tsp.	10 mL
Paprika	1/2 tsp.	2 mL
Chili powder	1 tsp.	5 mL

Combine all 9 ingredients in cloth bag or jar. Makes 2 cups (500 mL).

Pictured on page 123.

DIRECTIONS FOR

Spanish Rice: Empty contents of bag into large saucepan. Add 28 oz. (796 mL) can of diced tomatoes with juice, 1 3/4 cups (425 mL) water and 1 tbsp. (15 mL) hard margarine (or butter). Bring to a boil. Reduce heat. Cover. Simmer for about 25 minutes until rice is tender. Makes 7 cups (1.75 L).

1 cup (250 mL): 254 Calories; 2.5 g Total Fat; 293 mg Sodium; 5 g Protein; 53 g Carbohydrate; 2 g Dietary Fiber

Lemon Dill Rice Mix

This savory rice is the perfect partner to fish and seafood.

Long grain white rice, uncooked	2 cups	500 mL
Dill weed	2 tsp.	10 mL
Finely chopped dried chives	2 tsp.	10 mL
Vegetable (or chicken) bouillon powder	1 1/2 tbsp.	25 mL
Salt	1/2 tsp.	2 mL

Combine all 5 ingredients in cloth bag or jar. Makes 2 1/4 cups (550 mL).

Pictured on page 123.

DIRECTIONS FOR

Lemon Dill Rice: Empty contents of bag into large saucepan. Add 4 cups (1 L) water, 2 tbsp. (30 mL) lemon juice and 1 tbsp. (15 mL) hard margarine (or butter). Bring to a boil. Reduce heat. Cover. Simmer for about 20 minutes until rice is tender. Makes 7 cups (1.75 L).

1 cup (250 mL): 227 Calories; 2.4 g Total Fat; 611 mg Sodium; 4 g Protein; 46 g Carbohydrate; 1 g Dietary Fiber

Yellow Rice Mix

Brighten up your plate with this mild yet exotic rice mix.

Long grain white rice, uncooked	1 1/4 cups	300 mL
Beef bouillon powder	1 tsp.	5 mL
Minced onion flakes	1/4 cup	60 mL
Parsley flakes	1 tsp.	5 mL
Salt	1/2 tsp.	2 mL
Pepper	1/4 tsp.	1 mL
Turmeric	1/4 tsp.	1 mL

Combine all 7 ingredients in cloth bag or jar. Makes 1 1/2 cups (375 mL).

Pictured on page 123.

DIRECTIONS FOR

Yellow Rice: Empty contents of bag into medium saucepan. Add 2 1/2 cups (625 mL) water and 1 tbsp. (15 mL) hard margarine (or butter). Bring to a boil. Reduce heat. Cover. Simmer for about 20 minutes until rice is tender. Makes 4 cups (1 L).

1 cup (250 mL): 264 Calories; 3.4 g Total Fat; 483 mg Sodium; 5 g Protein; 52 g Carbohydrate; 1 g Dietary Fiber

Gift-Giving Soup Mix

The layers are so eye-catching. Choose a taller jar for best visual effect. The soup is wholesome and hearty.

Beef bouillon powder	1/4 cup	60 mL
Red lentils	1/4 cup	60 mL
Vegetable soup flakes	1/4 cup	60 mL
Pearl barley	1/4 cup	60 mL
Very small bow pasta	1/4 cup	60 mL
Yellow split peas	1/4 cup	60 mL
Wild rice	1/4 cup	60 mL

Layer all 7 ingredients, in order given, in jar. Makes about 1 1/2 cups (375 mL).

Pictured on front cover.

DIRECTIONS FOR

Gift-Giving Soup: Combine contents of jar and 7 cups (1.75 L) water in large pot or Dutch oven. Bring to a boil. Reduce heat. Cover. Simmer for about 50 minutes until peas and rice are tender. Add salt and pepper to taste. Makes about 7 1/2 cups (1.9 L).

1 cup (250 mL): 139 Calories; 1.2 g Total Fat; 1396 mg Sodium; 7 g Protein; 26 g Carbohydrate; 2 g Dietary Fiber

(In Bowls) Left: Yellow Rice Mix, page 122

Center: Spinach Rice Mix, page 122

Right: Lemon Dill Rice Mix, page 122
(In Jar) Right: Bean Soup Mix, this page

Bean Soup Mix

A hearty soup with a mild tomato and chili pepper flavor.

Dried red lentils	1/4 cup	60 mL
Dried baby lima beans	1/4 cup	60 mL
Dried black beans	1/4 cup	60 mL
Dried green lentils	1/4 cup	60 mL
Dried small red beans	1/4 cup	60 mL
Dried black-eyed peas	1/4 cup	60 mL
Dried pinto beans	1/4 cup	60 mL
Dried green split peas	1/4 cup	60 mL
Dried red kidney beans	1/4 cup	60 mL
Dried sweet basil	1 tsp.	5 mL
Parsley flakes	1 tbsp.	15 mL
Beef bouillon powder	1 tbsp.	15 mL
Bay leaf	1	1
Ground oregano	1 tsp.	5 mL
Salt	1 tsp.	5 mL

Layer first 9 ingredients, in order given, in jar.

Combine remaining 6 ingredients on piece of plastic wrap. Tie with twist tie or ribbon. Place on top of kidney bean layer. Secure lid. Makes about 2 cups (500 mL).

Pictured above.

DIRECTIONS FOR

Bean Soup: Empty contents of jar into large pot or Dutch oven. Rinse well and drain. Add 6 cups (1.5 L) hot water. Bring to a boil. Boil for 2 minutes. Remove from heat. Cover. Let stand for 1 hour. Drain. Rinse. Drain. Add 7 cups (1.75 L) water, 14 oz. (398 mL) can of Mexican stewed tomatoes with juice and packet of spice mix. Cook, stirring occasionally, for about 1 hour. Makes about 9 cups (2.25 L).

1 cup (250 mL): 174 Calories; 0.6 g Total Fat; 468 mg Sodium; 12 g Protein; 31 g Carbohydrate; 5 g Dietary Fiber

Southern Popcorn Mix

*This mixture of spices and seasonings delivers
a slightly sweet and mildly hot barbecue flavor.*

Chili powder	1 tsp.	5 mL
Envelope of spaghetti sauce mix	1 1/2 oz.	43 g
Granulated sugar	1 tsp.	5 mL
Garlic salt	1/2 tsp.	2 mL
Cayenne pepper	1/4 tsp.	1 mL

Combine all 5 ingredients in small bowl. Spoon into small
jar with tight-fitting lid. Makes about 1/2 cup (125 mL).

Pictured on page 125.

DIRECTIONS FOR

*Southern Popcorn: Melt 3 tbsp. (50 mL) hard margarine (or
butter) in small saucepan. Stir in 1 tbsp. (15 mL) Southern
Popcorn Mix. Drizzle over about 6 cups (1.5 L) popped corn
(1/4 cup, 60 mL, unpopped) in large bowl. Toss to coat well.*

*1 cup (250 mL): 88 Calories; 6.2 g Total Fat; 170 mg Sodium; 1 g Protein;
7 g Carbohydrate; 1 g Dietary Fiber*

Chili Cheese Popcorn Mix

A quick, light snack with a lot of kick.

Chili powder	1 1/2 tsp.	7 mL
Powdered Cheddar cheese product	1/3 cup	75 mL
Garlic salt	1 tsp.	5 mL
Cayenne pepper	1/8 tsp.	0.5 mL

Combine chili powder, cheese, garlic salt and cayenne
pepper in small bowl. Spoon into small jar with tight-fitting
lid. Makes 1/3 cup (75 mL).

Pictured on page 125.

DIRECTIONS FOR

*Chili Cheese Popcorn: Melt 2 tbsp. (30 mL) hard margarine
(or butter) in small saucepan. Drizzle over about 6 cups (1.5 L)
popped corn (1/4 cup, 60 mL, unpopped) in large bowl. Sprinkle
with 1 1/2 tbsp. (25 mL) Chili Cheese Popcorn Mix. Toss to
coat well.*

*1 cup (250 mL): 75 Calories; 4.8 g Total Fat; 112 mg Sodium; 2 g Protein;
7 g Carbohydrate; 1 g Dietary Fiber*

Chocolate Popcorn Mix

A nice way to satisfy a sweet and savory craving.

Icing (confectioner's) sugar	1 1/2 cups	375 mL
Cocoa, sifted if lumpy	1/2 cup	125 mL
Ground cinnamon (optional)	1/2 tsp.	2 mL

Combine all 3 ingredients in medium bowl. Spoon into jar
with tight-fitting lid. Makes about 2 cups (500 mL).

Pictured on page 125.

DIRECTIONS FOR

*Chocolate Popcorn: Melt 1/4 cup (60 mL) hard margarine (or
butter) in small saucepan. Stir in 1/4 cup (60 mL) Chocolate
Popcorn Mix. Drizzle over about 6 cups (1.5 L) popped corn
(1/4 cup, 60 mL, unpopped) in large bowl. Toss to coat well.*

*1 cup (250 mL): 124 Calories; 8.6 g Total Fat; 96 mg Sodium; 1 g Protein;
11 g Carbohydrate; 2 g Dietary Fiber*

Mexican Popcorn Mix

*Mexican chili meets Old World oregano
and basil in this full-bodied seasoning.*

Envelope of taco seasoning mix	1 1/4 oz.	35 g
Dried whole oregano, crushed	1 tsp.	5 mL
Dried sweet basil	1/2 tsp.	2 mL
Garlic powder	3/4 tsp.	4 mL

Combine seasoning mix, oregano, basil and garlic powder
in small bowl. Spoon into small jar with tight-fitting lid.
Makes about 1/3 cup (75 mL).

Pictured on page 125.

DIRECTIONS FOR

*Mexican Popcorn: Melt 3 tbsp. (50 mL) hard margarine (or
butter) in small saucepan. Drizzle over about 6 cups (1.5 L)
popped corn (1/4 cup, 60 mL, unpopped) in large bowl. Sprinkle
with 1 tbsp. (15 mL) Mexican Popcorn Mix. Toss to coat well.*

*1 cup (250 mL): 87 Calories; 6.2 g Total Fat; 188 mg Sodium; 1 g Protein;
7 g Carbohydrate; 1 g Dietary Fiber*

Clockwise from center:

Mexican Popcorn Mix, above
Chocolate Popcorn Mix, this page
Southern Popcorn Mix, this page
Chili Cheese Popcorn Mix, above

Chocolate
Popcorn Mix

Mexican
Popcorn
mix
See directions →

POPCORN

Chili Cheese
Popcorn Mix

Southern
Popcorn Mix
See directions

Authentic Indian Chai Tea Mix

"Masala" is the word for "spice" in India—hence "tea masala" is "spice for tea." Check out all of the interesting products!

Granulated sugar	1/4 cup	60 mL
Tea masala (available in South Asian grocery store)	1 tbsp.	15 mL
Whole loose black tea	1/3 cup	75 mL
Whole green cardamom	1/4 cup	60 mL
Cinnamon sticks, broken up	2/3 cup	150 mL
Chopped dried gingerroot	3 tbsp.	50 mL

Layer all 6 ingredients, in order given, in jar with tight-fitting lid. Makes about 1 1/2 cups (375 mL).

Pictured on page 127.

DIRECTIONS FOR

Authentic Indian Chai Tea: To Store: Pour contents of jar into plastic bag. Seal or close with twist tie while pushing excess air out. Lay bag on flat surface. Roll rolling pin over bag several times to break up cardamom pods. Return contents of bag to jar. Store in cool, dark place for up to 1 month. Always stir or shake very well before measuring to be sure the ingredients are evenly distributed. To Serve: Combine 6 tbsp. (100 mL) Chai Tea Mix, 2 1/2 cups (625 mL) milk and 1/2 cup (125 mL) water in medium saucepan. Heat on medium, stirring occasionally, until boiling and rich, light brown in color. Strain. Serves 2.

1 serving: 187 Calories; 3.8 g Total Fat; 168 mg Sodium; 11 g Protein; 28 g Carbohydrate; 1 Dietary Fiber

Far East Tea Mix

Once prepared, this tea embodies the Indian Chai flavor but with an added bite.

Whole cardamom	2	2
Whole cloves	4	4
Cinnamon stick (4 inches, 10 cm, long), broken into pieces	1	1
Granulated sugar	2 tbsp.	30 mL
Powdered coffee whitener	1 tbsp.	15 mL
Ground ginger	1/4 tsp.	1 mL
Pepper	1/8 tsp.	0.5 mL
Orange pekoe tea bag	1	1

Grind or pulverize first 3 ingredients in mortar. Spoon into cloth bag or jar.

Add sugar, coffee whitener, ginger and pepper. Shake to combine well.

Add tea bag. Makes about 1/3 cup (75 mL).

Pictured on page 127.

DIRECTIONS FOR

Far East Tea: Remove tea bag. Empty contents of bag into medium saucepan. Add 3 cups (750 mL) water. Bring to a boil. Remove from heat. Cover. Let stand for 5 minutes. Return to heat. Bring to a boil. Remove from heat. Add tea bag. Cover. Let stand for 3 minutes. Strain. Serves 2.

1 serving: 83 Calories; 1.3 g Total Fat; 12 mg Sodium; 1 g Protein; 19 g Carbohydrate; trace Dietary Fiber

Spiced Tea Mix

A yummy sweet tea with just the right amount of spice.

Powdered orange juice crystals (such as Tang)	1/2 cup	125 mL
Granulated sugar	2/3 cup	150 mL
Powdered iced tea mix, with lemon	2 tbsp.	30 mL
Ground cinnamon	1/2 tsp.	2 mL
Ground cloves	1/4 tsp.	1 mL

Pour orange crystals into jar with tight-fitting lid.

Spoon sugar over orange crystals.

Combine tea, cinnamon and cloves in small cup. Spoon over orange crystals. Makes 1 1/4 cups (300 mL).

Pictured on page 127.

DIRECTIONS FOR

Spiced Tea: Stir contents of jar before measuring. Measure 2 tsp. (10 mL) into mug. Add 3/4 cup (175 mL) boiling water. Stir. Serves 1.

1 serving: 34 Calories; 0 g Total Fat; 1 mg Sodium; trace Protein; 9 g Carbohydrate; trace Dietary Fiber

Center Top: Spiced Tea Mix, above
Center Right: Authentic Indian Chai Tea Mix, this page
Center Left and Bottom: Far East Tea Mix, this page

Spiced
TEA
see back for
directions

Mochaccino Mix

Mix up a cup on a cold evening.

Powdered coffee whitener	3 tbsp.	50 mL
Granulated sugar	1/3 cup	75 mL
Instant coffee granules	1/4 cup	60 mL
Cocoa, sifted if lumpy	1/4 cup	60 mL
Skim milk powder	1 cup	250 mL

Combine all 5 ingredients in plastic bag or jar with tight-fitting lid. Makes 2 cups (500 mL).

Pictured on front cover.

DIRECTIONS FOR

Mochaccino: Measure 1/4 cup (60 mL) Mochaccino Mix into blender. Add 1 cup (250 mL) hot milk. Process, according to blender instructions for hot liquids, until smooth. Pour into mug. Top with whipped cream. Sprinkle with grated chocolate or cinnamon. Serves 1.

1 serving: 223 Calories; 4.1 g Total Fat; 219 mg Sodium; 15 g Protein; 33 g Carbohydrate; 1 g Dietary Fiber

Cappuccino Mix

Choose a jar that shows off the layers.

Instant chocolate drink powder	1 cup	250 mL
Powdered coffee whitener	1/2 cup	125 mL
Instant coffee granules	1/2 cup	125 mL
Skim milk powder	1/2 cup	125 mL
Ground cinnamon	1 tsp.	5 mL
Ground nutmeg	1/4 tsp.	1 mL

Layer all 6 ingredients, in order given, in jar with tight-fitting lid. Makes 2 1/4 cups (550 mL).

Pictured on page 129 and on page 115.

DIRECTIONS FOR

Cappuccino: Stir contents of jar before measuring. Measure 2 tbsp. (30 mL) Cappuccino Mix into blender. Add 1 cup (250 mL) boiling water. Process, according to blender instructions for hot liquids, until foamy. Pour into mug. Sprinkle with nutmeg. Serves 1.

1 serving: 65 Calories; 1.3 g Total Fat; 44 mg Sodium; 2 g Protein; 13 g Carbohydrate; trace Dietary Fiber

Café Latte Mix

A quick version of the coffee shop favorite.

Skim milk powder	2 cups	500 mL
Instant coffee granules	3 tbsp.	50 mL
Powdered coffee whitener	1/2 cup	125 mL

Combine all 3 ingredients in plastic bag or jar with tight-fitting lid. Makes about 2 1/3 cups (575 mL).

Pictured on page 129.

DIRECTIONS FOR

Café Latte: Measure 1/3 cup (75 mL) Café Latte Mix into blender. Add 1 cup (250 mL) boiling water. Process, according to blender instructions for hot liquids, until foamy. Pour into large mug. Sweeten to taste. Serves 1.

1 serving: 174 Calories; 2.8 g Total Fat; 207 mg Sodium; 14 g Protein; 23 g Carbohydrate; 0 g Dietary Fiber

Hot Choco Coffee Mix

A rich, creamy, foamy drink. A great drink to sip while reading a good book.

Granulated sugar	2/3 cup	150 mL
Cocoa	1/3 cup	75 mL
Ground cinnamon	1/4 tsp.	1 mL
Instant coffee granules	1/4 cup	60 mL

Measure sugar into small bowl. Sift cocoa, cinnamon and coffee granules into sugar. Stir. Spoon into plastic bag or jar with tight-fitting lid. Makes about 1 cup (250 mL).

Pictured on page 129 and on page 63.

DIRECTIONS FOR

Hot Choco Coffee: Heat 1 cup (250 mL) milk in large mug in microwave on high (100%) for about 2 minutes until very hot. Add 1 1/2 tbsp. (25 mL) Hot Choco Coffee Mix. Stir. Serves 1.

1 serving: 167 Calories; 3.1 g Total Fat; 130 mg Sodium; 9 g Protein; 27 g Carbohydrate; 1 g Dietary Fiber

Top: Café Latte Mix, above
Center Right and Bottom: Cappuccino Mix, this page
Bottom Left: Hot Choco Coffee Mix, above
Center: Nutty Biscotti, page 39

Café Latte

HOT CHOCO
COFFEE

Cappuccino
Mix

Banff

Hot Toddy Mix

Warms you from the inside out.

Hard margarine (or butter), softened	1/2 cup	125 mL
Dark brown sugar (not demerara), packed	3 cups	750 mL
Ground cinnamon	1/4 tsp.	1 mL
Ground nutmeg	1/4 tsp.	1 mL
Ground cloves	1/4 tsp.	1 mL

Cream margarine and brown sugar together in large bowl.

Add cinnamon, nutmeg and cloves. Mix. Spoon into jar with tight-fitting lid. Makes about 3 1/2 cups (875 mL).

Pictured on this page.

DIRECTIONS FOR

Hot Toddy: Measure 2 tbsp. (30 mL) Hot Toddy Mix into mug. Add 1 1/2 oz. (45 mL) dark rum. Fill mug with boiling water. Stir. Serves 1. Store remaining mix in refrigerator for up to 2 months.

1 serving: 249 Calories; 4.2 g Total Fat; 61 mg Sodium; trace Protein; 30 g Carbohydrate; trace Dietary Fiber

Top: Hot Toddy Mix, this page
Right: Grog and Coffee Mix, this page
Left: Mulled Apple Juice Mix, below

Grog And Coffee Mix

A sweet and spicy drink with a subtle taste of rum.

Hard margarine (or butter)	2 tbsp.	30 mL
Brown sugar, packed	1 cup	250 mL
Ground cinnamon	1/4 tsp.	1 mL
Ground nutmeg	1/8 tsp.	0.5 mL
Ground cloves	1/16 tsp.	0.5 mL
Instant coffee granules	2/3 cup	150 mL

Melt margarine in small saucepan. Remove from heat. Add remaining 5 ingredients. Mix thoroughly. Spoon into jar with tight-fitting lid. Makes 2 cups (500 mL).

Pictured on this page.

DIRECTIONS FOR

Grog And Coffee: Measure 1 tbsp. (15 mL) Grog And Coffee Mix into mug. Add 1 1/2 oz. (45 mL) light rum, 2 tbsp. (30 mL) heavy cream and strip of lemon and orange peel. Add 3/4 cup (175 mL) boiling water. Stir. Serves 1. Store remaining mix in refrigerator for up to 2 months.

1 serving: 170 Calories; 3.8 g Total Fat; 24 mg Sodium; 1 g Protein; 9 g Carbohydrate; trace Dietary Fiber

Mulled Apple Juice Mix

A good family drink to enjoy around the fire.

Cinnamon sticks, (about 7 inches, 18 cm, each), broken in half	12	12
Whole cloves	24	24
Whole allspice	24	24
Sugar cubes (optional)	6	6

Combine 4 cinnamon stick pieces, 4 cloves, 4 allspice and 1 sugar cube in 5 x 5 inch (12.5 x 12.5 cm) piece of double layer cheesecloth. Tie with ribbon or string. Repeat with remaining spices and cheesecloth. Makes 6 gift bags.

Pictured above.

DIRECTIONS FOR

Mulled Apple Juice: Drop 1 bag into 8 cups (2 L) apple juice in large saucepan. Cover. Simmer for 10 minutes. Keep hot, without simmering, for 1 1/2 hours. Remove and discard bag. Makes about 8 cups (2 L).

1 cup (250 mL): 124 Calories; 0.3 g Total Fat; 8 mg Sodium; trace Protein; 31 g Carbohydrate; trace Dietary Fiber

Liqueurs & Beverages

Liqueurs are the gift to give adults, but both young and old will enjoy the non-alcoholic beverages also featured in this section. With just a few ingredients, you can make a wonderful fruit-flavored liqueur to share with hosts and hostesses alike. Save bottles to use for these delightful concoctions, or look for especially pretty or unusual shaped bottles in stores and at flea markets. Dress up plain bottles with miniature fruit or a Bottle Apron, page 135. Some of these beverages can also be packaged in pitchers, plastic containers, bottles or jars.

Bloody Mary Concentrate, page 140

ESPECIALLY
FOR
YOUR
BRIDAL
SHOWER

Congratulations
Sherri & Neil

A
SHOWER
GIFT

Cranberry Liqueur

Pretty, deep red color. The bouquet will say "gin," but the taste will say "cranberry."

Fresh (or frozen) cranberries, coarsely chopped	4 cups	1 L
Granulated sugar	3 cups	750 mL
Gin	2 cups	500 mL
Vanilla	1 tsp.	5 mL

Combine all 4 ingredients in large jar with tight-fitting lid. Let stand at room temperature for 6 weeks, shaking jar well once a week. Strain and return to jar. Store in cool location. Makes 3 1/2 cups (875 L).

1/4 cup (60 mL): 259 Calories; 0.1 g Total Fat; 1 mg Sodium; trace Protein; 48 g Carbohydrate; 1 g Dietary Fiber

Pictured on page 133.

Grand Marnier

Dark amber color. True Grand Marnier flavor.

Finely grated orange zest (no white pith)	1/2 tbsp.	7 mL
Orange sections	1 cup	250 mL
Granulated sugar	1 cup	250 mL
Brown sugar, packed	1 cup	250 mL
Brandy	3/4 cup	175 mL

Combine first 4 ingredients in jar with tight-fitting lid. Pour brandy over top. Do not stir. Cover. Let stand at room temperature for 5 weeks. Strain and return to jar. Makes 2 1/3 cups (575 mL).

1/4 cup (60 mL): 169 Calories; 0 g Total Fat; 7 mg Sodium; trace Protein; 36 g Carbohydrate; trace Dietary Fiber

Pictured on page 132.

Plum Liqueur

Deep burgundy color with a nice plum flavor. Serve with club soda.

Black plums (about 8), chopped	1 1/2 lbs.	680 g
Granulated sugar	3 cups	750 mL
Vodka (or gin)	2 1/4 cups	550 mL

Put plums into large jar with tight-fitting lid. Pour sugar over top. Do not stir. Pour vodka over top. Do not stir. Let stand at room temperature for 3 months. Strain and return to jar. Makes 5 1/2 cups (1.4 L).

1/4 cup (60 mL): 175 Calories; 0 g Total fat; 2 mg Sodium; trace Protein; 31 g Carbohydrate; 0 g Dietary Fiber

Pictured on page 133 and page on 135.

Peach Liqueur

Beautiful, true shade of peach. Doesn't settle; stays nicely mixed.

Apricot nectar (two 8 oz., 225 mL boxes	16 oz.	500 mL
Sweetened peach drink powder	1 cup	250 mL
Can of frozen concentrated lemonade, thawed	12 1/2 oz.	355 mL
Vodka	2 cups	500 mL

Combine all 4 ingredients in large jar with tight-fitting lid. Stir. Store in refrigerator. Makes 6 cups (1.5 L).

1/4 cup (60 mL): 97 Calories; 0.1 g Total Fat; 4 mg Sodium; trace Protein; 13 g Carbohydrate; trace Dietary Fiber

Pictured on page 133.

Variation: Peach Liqueur Sparkler: Pour 1/4 cup (60 mL) Peach Liqueur over ice. Add 1/2 cup (125 mL) club soda or sparkling water. Serves 1.

Photo Legend previous page from left to right:

Grand Marnier, above
Cranberry Liqueur, above
Plum Liqueur, this page
Peach Liqueur, this page

How To

Bottle Apron

You've spent time making a special bottle of liqueur or wine. Now make it eyecatching with an apron of its own. This pattern is easily reduced or enlarged to fit any size of bottle.

Plum Liqueur, page 134

1 square = 1 inch (2.5 cm)

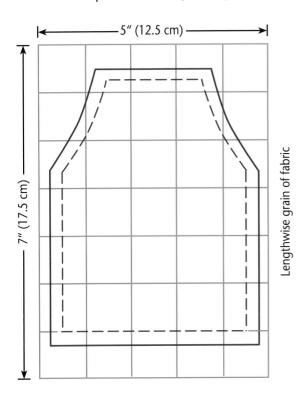

5" (12.5 cm)

7" (17.5 cm)

Lengthwise grain of fabric

Materials: Piece of brown paper at least 4 × 5 inches (10 × 12.5 cm), pencil, ruler, scissors, pins, 5 × 7 inch (12.5 × 17.5 cm) piece of material, iron, sewing machine, matching thread, measuring tape, double-fold bias tape.

1. To enlarge pattern, above, mark 1 inch (2.5 cm) squares on brown paper. Transfer pattern to grid, matching lines within each square. Cut out pattern.

2. Pin pattern to right side of material. Cut out.

3. Press under 1/4 inch (6 mm) seam allowance along top, sides and bottom, leaving armholes. Sew seam allowance 1/8 inch (3 mm) from edge.

4. Measure two 18 inch (45 cm) pieces of double-fold bias tape. Leaving 6 inches (11.5 cm) at top of one piece of bias tape for tie, pin tape to apron along arm area, encasing raw edge.

5. Sew tape close to inside edge along entire length. Be sure to catch apron material at arm area. Repeat for other side.

Amaretto

Thin, golden liquid with an classic almond flavor.

Granulated sugar	2 cups	500 mL
Boiling water	1 1/2 cups	375 mL
Vodka	2 cups	500 mL
Brandy	2 cups	500 mL
Almond flavoring	1 1/2 tbsp.	25 mL

Bring sugar and water to a boil in large saucepan. Boil for 2 minutes. Cool for about 30 minutes.

Add vodka, brandy and almond flavoring. Stir. Pour into jar with tight-fitting lid. Store at room temperature for at least 1 week before serving. Makes 6 cups (1.5 L).

1/4 cup (60 mL): 159 Calories; 0 g Total Fat; 1 mg Sodium; 0 g Protein; 18 g Carbohydrate; 0 g Dietary Fiber

Pictured on this page.

DIRECTIONS FOR

Amaretto: Can be stored at room temperature for up to 3 weeks.

Kahlúa, below   Amaretto, this page   Irish Cream, this page

Irish Cream

Irish-creamy good! Takes only 2 minutes to make.

Can of sweetened condensed milk	11 oz.	300 mL
Large eggs	3	3
Can of skim evaporated milk	13 1/2 oz.	385 mL
Milk	1/4 cup	60 mL
Instant chocolate drink powder	1 tbsp.	15 mL
Coconut flavoring	1/8 tsp.	0.5 mL
Instant coffee granules, crushed	1 tsp.	5 mL
Irish (or rye) whiskey	1 cup	250 mL

Put first 7 ingredients into blender. Blend until smooth.

Add whiskey. Mix. Pour into jar with tight-fitting lid. Store in refrigerator. Makes 5 cups (1.25 L).

1/4 cup (60 mL): 122 Calories; 2.6 g Total Fat; 62 mg Sodium; 4 g Protein; 14 g Carbohydrate; 0 g Dietary Fiber

Pictured on this page.

DIRECTIONS FOR

Irish Cream: Can be stored in refrigerator for up to 3 weeks.

Kahlúa

Dark brown and syrupy. Coffee and vanilla flavors balance the sweetness.

Granulated sugar	4 cups	1 L
Instant coffee granules	1/4 cup	60 mL
Boiling water	2 1/4 cups	550 mL
Brandy	2 cups	500 mL
Vanilla beans	2	2

Stir sugar, coffee granules and boiling water in pitcher or large bowl. Stir until sugar is dissolved. Cool.

Add brandy and vanilla beans. Stir. Cover. Let stand at room temperature for about 20 days. Strain into jar with tight-fitting lid. Makes 6 1/4 cups (1.5 L).

1/4 cup (60 mL): 174 Calories; trace Total Fat; 2 mg Sodium; trace Protein; 34 g Carbohydrate; 0 g Dietary Fiber

Pictured above.

Spiced Red Wine

Takes red wine to new heights! Spicy sweetness.

Dry (or alcohol-free) red wine	3 cups	750 mL
Granulated sugar	1/4 cup	60 mL
Cinnamon sticks (about 7 inches, 18 cm, each), broken into pieces	2	2
Whole cloves	3	3
Dried orange peel	2 tsp.	10 mL

Combine all 5 ingredients in saucepan. Heat slowly, stirring often. Simmer for 15 to 20 minutes to release spice flavors. Strain into jar with tight-fitting lid. Can be served warm or chilled. Makes 2 1/3 cups (575 mL).

1/2 cup (125 mL): 161 Calories; 0 g Total Fat; 8 mg Sodium; trace Protein; 15 g Carbohydrate; trace Dietary Fiber

Pictured on this page.

Strawberry Wine

Lovely, dark rose color. This is probably about a 2 to 3 in sweetness.

Dry (or alcohol-free) white wine	3 cups	750 mL
Granulated sugar	1/4 cup	60 mL
Sliced fresh strawberries	2 cups	500 mL

Combine wine and sugar in pitcher or medium bowl. Stir until sugar is dissolved.

Add strawberries. Stir. Cover. Let stand in refrigerator for 3 days. Strain into jar with tight-fitting lid. Makes 3 cups (750 mL).

1/2 cup (125 mL): 137 Calories; 0.2 g Total Fat; 7 mg Sodium; trace Protein; 14 g Carbohydrate; 1 g Dietary Fiber

Pictured on this page.

Back: Spiced Red Wine, above
Front: Strawberry Wine, above

Ginger Tea Syrup

Take this along to your next picnic. Just add cold water and ice for a refreshing summer drink.

Water	4 cups	1 L
Granulated sugar	2 cups	500 mL
Finely chopped gingerroot	1 tbsp.	15 mL
Grated lemon peel	2 tsp.	10 mL
Black tea bags (such as) orange pekoe	8	8
Lemon juice	6 tbsp.	100 mL

Bring water, sugar, ginger and lemon peel to a boil in medium saucepan. Boil for 10 minutes.

Add tea bags. Stir. Let stand for 10 minutes, stirring occasionally, until tea is very dark.

Strain into pitcher or bowl. Stir in lemon juice. Pour into jar with tight-fitting lid. Makes 4 cups (1 L).

Pictured on page 139.

DIRECTIONS FOR

Ginger Tea: Add 1 part syrup to 3 parts water, over ice cubes. Syrup can be stored in refrigerator for up to 2 weeks.

1/3 cup (75 mL) syrup only: 141 Calories; 0 g Total Fat; 6 mg Sodium; trace Protein; 36 g Carbohydrate; trace Dietary Fiber

Fruit Punch Concentrate

So handy to make one glass at a time.

Water	4 cups	1 L
Granulated sugar	2 cups	500 mL
Package of sweetened raspberry-flavored drink mix	7 1/2 oz.	210 g
Package of unsweetened grape-flavored drink mix	1/4 oz.	8 g
Package of unsweetened lemon-flavored drink mix	1/4 oz.	8 g

Bring water and sugar to a boil in medium saucepan. Boil for 1 minute.

Add remaining 3 ingredients. Stir until dissolved. Bring to a boil. Boil for 10 minutes. Cool. Pour into jar with tight-fitting lid. Makes 5 cups (1.25 L) flavoring.

Pictured on page 139.

DIRECTIONS FOR

Fruit Punch: Add 1 part concentrate to 4 parts of either club soda or lemon-lime soft drink, over ice cubes.

1/4 cup (60 mL) concentrate only: 122 Calories; trace Total Fat; 13 mg Sodium; 0 g Protein; 32 g Carbohydrate; 0 g Dietary Fiber

Citrus Drink Concentrate

Equal tartness and sweetness. Makes a large recipe for several gifts.

Citric acid (see Note)	1/4 cup	60 mL
Epsom salts (see Note)	2 tbsp.	30 mL
Granulated sugar	11 cups	2.75 L
Boiling water	6 cups	1.5 L
Tartaric acid (see Note)	2 tbsp.	30 mL
Finely grated orange zest	3 tbsp.	50 mL
Finely grated lemon zest	2 tbsp.	30 mL
Freshly squeezed orange juice (about 3 large)	1 1/2 cups	375 mL
Freshly squeezed lemon juice (about 3 large)	1 cup	250 mL

Combine all 9 ingredients in large glass bowl. Stir for 2 to 3 minutes until sugar is dissolved. Let stand for 1 hour. Strain into jars with tight-fitting lids. Store in refrigerator. Makes 14 cups (3.5 L).

Pictured on page 139.

Lemonade variation: Omit oranges and make with 6 lemons. This recipe halves easily.

Note: Citric acid, Epsom salts and tartaric acid can be found at a pharmacy or health food store.

DIRECTIONS FOR

Citrus Drink: Add 1 part concentrate to 3 or 4 parts water, over ice cubes.

1/3 cup (75 mL) concentrate only: 221 Calories; 0 g Total Fat; 337 mg Sodium; trace Protein; 57 g Carbohydrate; trace Dietary Fiber

Left: Fruit Punch Concentrate, this page
Center: Ginger Tea Syrup, this page
Right: Citrus Drink Concentrate, above

Fruit Punch Concentrate
see back for directions

Ginger Tea Syrup
see back for directions

Christmas Citrus Drink
see back for directions

Splash time!

Bloody Mary Concentrate

More orange than red. Fresh flavor with a nip from the cayenne pepper.

Large ripe tomatoes, sliced	15	15
Chopped onion	3 cups	750 mL
Prepared horseradish	2 tbsp.	30 mL
Granulated sugar	1/4 cup	60 mL
White vinegar	1/4 cup	60 mL
Celery salt	1/2 tsp.	2 mL
Cayenne pepper	1/4–1/2 tsp.	1–2 mL
Garlic powder	1/2 tsp.	2 mL
Salt	2 tsp.	10 mL
Pepper	1/4 tsp.	1 mL
Tomato paste	1/4 cup	60 mL

Put all 11 ingredients into large pot or Dutch oven. Bring to a boil, stirring often. Reduce heat. Cover. Simmer gently for 30 to 40 minutes, stirring occasionally. Strain. Cool. Pour into large plastic container, leaving 1 inch (2.5 cm) at top. Cover. Freeze. Makes 6 cups (1.5 L).

Pictured on this page and on page 131.

DIRECTIONS FOR

Bloody Mary: Measure 1 1/2 oz. (45 mL) vodka into old fashioned glass. Add 3 ice cubes. Fill with about 3/4 cup (175 mL) thawed Bloody Mary Concentrate. Serves 1.

1 serving: 207 Calories; 1 g Total Fat; 702 mg Sodium; 3 g Protein; 26 g Carbohydrate; 4 g Dietary Fiber

Mock Champagne Concentrate, below   Bloody Mary Concentrate, this page

Mock Champagne Concentrate

Just add ginger ale or soda water to make the bubbles!

Apple juice	2 cups	500 mL
Granulated sugar	1/2 cup	125 mL
Lemon juice	1/2 cup	125 mL
Can of frozen concentrated white grape juice, thawed	12 oz.	341 mL

Bring apple juice and sugar to a boil in small saucepan. Boil, uncovered, for 10 minutes.

Add lemon juice and grape juice. Stir well. Fill jars or bottles for gift-giving. Makes 3 2/3 cups (900 mL) champagne concentrate.

Pictured above.

DIRECTIONS FOR

Mock Champagne: Measure 1 cup (250 mL) champagne concentrate into pitcher. Add 2 cups (500 mL) ginger ale or club soda. Makes 3 cups (750 mL), enough for 4 servings. Keep remaining concentrate in refrigerator for up to 2 weeks.

1 serving: 141 Calories; 0.1 g Total Fat; 12 mg Sodium; trace Protein; 36 g Carbohydrate; trace Dietary Fiber

Snacks

Satisfy cravings for sweet or salty snacks with these gifts of food to eat by the handful. Turn any variety of nuts into a tantalizing treat. Make out-of-the-ordinary chips from yams, bagels or tortillas. Transform cereal, crackers and dried fruit into savory sweet treats to take on long trips in the car or to fill the hunger gap at school. Be sure to dress up your snacks in neat jars, bags and tins—you'll find some creative decorating suggestions on pages 146 and 147.

Spiced Nuts, page 148

Cracker
Snack
Mix

BOX

Spicy Oriental Mix

Lots of different shapes, textures and flavors.
This mix features a lingering spicy nip.

Package of rice crackers, broken up	16 oz.	500 g
Almonds	1 cup	250 mL
Pretzels	8 cups	2 L
Packages of instant Chinese noodles (3 oz., 85 g, each), broken up and flavor packet discarded	2	2
Soy sauce	1/2 cup	125 mL
Dried crushed chilies	1/2–1 tsp.	2–5 mL
Ground ginger	1/2 tsp.	2 mL
Garlic powder	1/2 tsp.	2 mL
Worcestershire sauce	1 tsp.	5 mL
Hoisin sauce	1 tsp.	5 mL
Granulated sugar	1/2 tsp.	2 mL

Combine first 4 ingredients in roasting pan.

Combine remaining 7 ingredients in small bowl. Pour over cracker mixture. Toss until well coated. Bake in 275°F (140°C) oven for 30 minutes until crispy. Stir. Bake for 15 to 20 minutes. Makes 20 cups (5 L).

1/2 cup (125 mL): 152 Calories; 8.7 g Total Fat; 513 mg Sodium; 5 g Protein; 15 g Carbohydrate; 1 g Dietary Fiber

Pictured on page 142.

Smoked Almonds

Crisp nuts with salty coating.
A great nibbler with liquid refreshments.

Cooking oil	1 tbsp.	15 mL
Whole almonds, with skin	1 cup	250 mL
Liquid smoke	1 tsp.	5 mL
All-purpose flour	2 tsp.	10 mL
Sea salt	1 tsp.	5 mL

Photo Legend previous page
from left to right:

Spicy Oriental Mix, above
Nuts And Bolts, this page
Smoked Almonds, above
Cracker Snack Mix, page 145

Pour cooking oil over almonds in small bowl. Toss to coat well. Spread on ungreased baking sheet. Bake in 275°F (140°C) oven for 45 minutes.

Remove from oven. Pour nuts into medium bowl. Sprinkle with liquid smoke. Toss to coat well.

Mix flour and salt in cup. Sprinkle over almonds. Toss to coat well. Spread on same baking sheet. Bake for 20 minutes. Cool. Makes 1 cup (250 mL).

2 tbsp. (30 mL): 123 Calories; 11.1 g Total Fat; 287 mg Sodium; 4 g Protein; 4 g Carbohydrate; 1 g Dietary Fiber

Pictured on page 142/143.

Nuts And Bolts

A popular mix with everyone—makes enough for four generous gifts.

O-shaped toasted oat cereal	12 cups	3 L
Whole wheat squares cereal	7 cups	1.75 L
Pretzels (regular or stick)	9 cups	2.25 L
Mixed nuts (or your favorite)	3 cups	750 mL
Hard margarine (or butter)	1 1/2 cups	375 mL
Worcestershire sauce	2 tbsp.	30 mL
Garlic salt	2 tsp.	10 mL
Celery salt	2 tsp.	10 mL
Seasoned salt	2 tsp.	10 mL

Combine both cereals, pretzels and nuts in large roasting pan.

Melt margarine in medium saucepan. Add remaining 4 ingredients. Stir. Drizzle over cereal mixture. Toss to coat well. Bake, uncovered, in 250°F (120°C) oven for about 2 hours, stirring every 30 minutes. Cool. Store in airtight container. Makes 31 cups (7.75 L).

1/2 cup (125 mL): 152 Calories; 9 g Total Fat; 421 mg Sodium; 3 g Protein; 16 g Carbohydrate; 2 g Dietary Fiber

Pictured on page 142.

Beef Jerky

Not too salty, not too smoky—just right!
Texture ranges from chewy to crispy.

Lean beef (such as rump, top round or sirloin), 1 inch (2.5 cm) thick, completely trimmed of fat	2 lbs.	900 g
Soy sauce	1/3 cup	75 mL
Worcestershire sauce	2 tbsp.	30 mL
Onion powder	1/2 tsp.	2 mL
Garlic powder	1/2 tsp.	2 mL
Ground ginger	1/2 tsp.	2 mL
Salt	1 tsp.	5 mL
Pepper	1/4 tsp.	1 mL
Granulated sugar	1 tbsp.	15 mL
Liquid smoke	1/2 tsp.	2 mL

Cut beef into 1/8 inch (3 mm) slices. Cut slices as long as possible. Cutting with the grain results in chewy jerky. Cutting across the grain results in tender, crunchy jerky.

Combine remaining 9 ingredients in medium bowl. Stir until sugar dissolves. Add beef. Stir to coat well. Cover. Chill overnight. Set wire racks in foil-lined baking pans with sides. Draw beef strips across edge of bowl to remove excess marinade. Arrange in single layer close together on racks. Bake in 170°F (75°C) oven for 6 to 7 hours, turning over strips at half-time and rearranging pans, until beef strips are browned, hard and dried. Store in air-tight container. If moisture forms inside storage container, bake once more for a short time. Makes 1 lb. (454 g).

2 oz. (57 g): 152 calories; 4.3 g Total Fat; 883 mg Sodium; 24 g Protein; 3 g Carbohydrate; trace Dietary Fiber

Pictured on this page.

TURKEY JERKY: Simply use white meat from turkey rather than beef.

Cracker Snack Mix

Shades of gold in this handy-to-have-on-hand snack mix.

Oyster crackers	2 cups	500 mL
Whole wheat squares cereal	2 cups	500 mL
Dry-roasted peanuts	2 cups	500 mL
Sesame seeds	1/3 cup	75 mL
Hard margarine (or butter), melted	1/2 cup	125 mL
Beef bouillon powder	1 tbsp.	15 mL
Minced onion flakes	2 tbsp.	30 mL
Onion powder	1/2 tsp.	2 mL

Combine first 4 ingredients in large bowl.

Combine remaining 4 ingredients in small saucepan. Drizzle over cracker mixture. Stir to coat well. Spread on ungreased 11 × 17 inch (28 × 43 cm) baking sheet. Bake in 350°F (175°C) oven for about 15 minutes, stirring once, until lightly browned. Cool. Store in airtight container. Makes 7 cups (1.75 L).

1/2 cup (125 mL): 271 Calories; 20.6 g Total Fat; 517 mg Sodium; 7 g Protein; 17 g Carbohydrate; 4 g Dietary Fiber

Pictured on page 143.

Beef Jerky, this page

How To

Stenciled Toolbox

When you want to personalize an item, stencils are the answer. Remember that your brush should not be loaded with paint or it will bleed under the stencil.

Materials: Toolbox, stencil tape, stencils, sponge brush, acrylic paint for metal, paper towel.

1. Make sure surface is clean. Use stencil tape to mark off lines along top of where you want lettering. Align stencil with bottom edge of tape. Affix with stencil tape. Dip sponge brush into paint. Dab excess paint onto paper towel. Dab paint onto stencil.

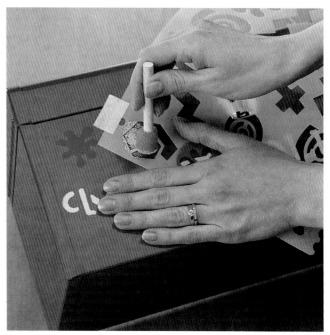

2. Affix decorative stencil tape where desired. Paint.

3. A variety of stencils are available at scrapbooking and craft stores. Alternatively, cut your own from a piece of mylar, a thick plastic available in craft stores.

How To

Nuts And Bolts Lid

Give Nuts And Bolts, page 144, to someone in a customized jar they can later use for trinkets around the house or in the workshop.

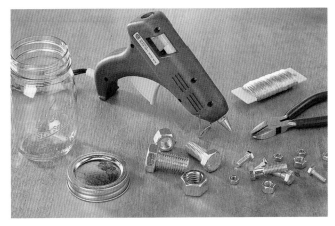

Materials: Jar with lid, glue gun, assorted sizes of nuts and bolts, 26-gauge wire, wire cutters.

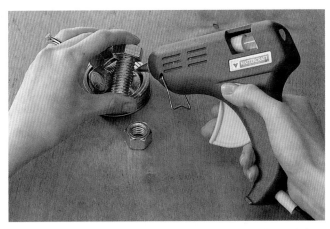

1. If lid is in two pieces, glue lid rim to lid center for stability. Glue large nuts and bolts onto lid.

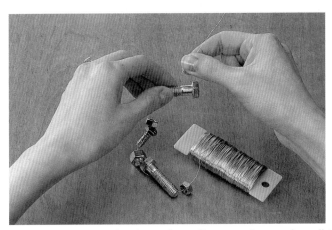

2. Wrap 26-gauge wire through small nuts and around small bolts, leaving 1 inch (2.5 cm) at each end. Form to fit neck of jar. Secure by twisting ends of wire together.

Snack Mix Lid

For a fun gift, decorate a jar of snack mix (your choice, page 144 to 154) with some of the ingredients. After the treat is gone, the jar will fit into most kitchen décors.

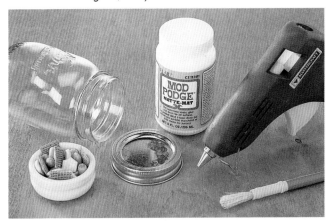

Materials: Jar with lid, glue gun, snack mix, paintbrush, clear-drying white glue.

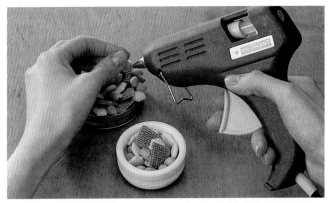

1. If lid is in two pieces, glue lid rim to lid center with glue gun for stability. Glue snack mix pieces onto lid with glue gun, starting on outside and working your way in a circular pattern to the inside.

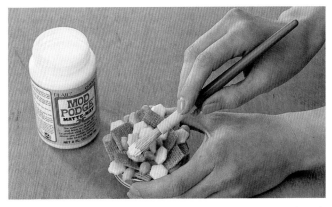

2. Brush entire top of lid with white glue to protect and seal.

Curried Almonds

Almonds soften slightly because of the coating.
Pleasant curry flavor.

Hard margarine (or butter)	1 1/2 tbsp.	25 mL
Blanched whole almonds	2 cups	500 mL
Curry paste (available in Asian section of grocery store)	1/2 tbsp.	7 mL
Salt	3/4 tsp.	4 mL

Melt margarine in 9 x 9 inch (22 x 22 cm) pan. Add almonds. Stir to coat well. Bake in 300°F (150°C) oven for about 30 minutes, stirring 2 or 3 times.

Add curry paste and salt. Toss to coat well. Turn out onto waxed paper to cool. Store in airtight container. Makes 2 cups (500 mL).

1/2 cup (125 mL): 509 Calories; 46.9 g Total Fat; 509 mg Sodium; 16 g Protein; 14 g Carbohydrate; 9 g Dietary Fiber

Pictured on page 149.

Spiced Nuts

Crusty on the outside but sweet nonetheless.

Brown sugar, packed	1/2 cup	125 mL
Granulated sugar	1/2 cup	125 mL
Ground cinnamon	1 1/2 tsp.	7 mL
Ground nutmeg	1/2 tsp.	2 mL
Ground ginger	1/2 tsp.	2 mL
Ground cloves	1/4 tsp.	1 mL
Egg white (large)	1	1
Water	1 tbsp.	15 mL
Mixed nuts	4 cups	1 L

Combine first 6 ingredients in small bowl.

Beat egg white and water in medium bowl until frothy. Add sugar mixture. Stir.

Add nuts. Stir. Spread on greased baking sheet. Bake in 325°F (160°C) oven for 20 minutes, stirring occasionally, until golden. Cool thoroughly. Store in airtight container. Makes 6 cups (1.5 L).

1/2 cup (125 mL): 327 Calories; 25.8 g Total Fat; 9 mg Sodium; 3 g Protein; 26 g Carbohydrate; 3 g Dietary Fiber

Pictured on page 149 and on page 141.

Roasted Pecans

Crispy, generous coating with just
a hint of sweetness from the ketchup.

Hard margarine (or butter)	1 tbsp.	15 mL
Ketchup	2 tsp.	10 mL
Worcestershire sauce	2 tbsp.	30 mL
Cayenne pepper	1/4 tsp.	1 mL
Pecans	2 cups	500 mL

Salt, sprinkle

Melt margarine in large saucepan. Add next 4 ingredients. Stir to coat well. Spread on greased baking sheet. Bake in 350°F (175°C) oven for 20 minutes, stirring every 5 minutes. Turn out onto paper towel.

Sprinkle with salt. Makes 2 cups (500 mL).

1/2 cup (125 mL): 414 Calories; 41.5 g Total Fat; 157 mg Sodium; 5 g Protein; 12 g Carbohydrate; 4 Dietary Fiber

Pictured on page 149.

Orange Fudgey Pecans

The coating is definitely fudge-like. Yummy!

Pecan halves	3 cups	750 mL
Grated orange peel	1 tbsp.	15 mL
Granulated sugar	1 1/2 cups	375 mL
Prepared orange juice	1/2 cup	125 mL
Milk	1/2 cup	125 mL

Measure pecans into large glass bowl. Add orange peel.

Combine sugar, orange juice and milk in large saucepan. Heat and stir until sugar is dissolved and mixture is boiling. Boil, without stirring, until mixture reaches soft ball stage (234° to 240°F, 112° to 116°C) on candy thermometer or until small amount dropped into very cold water forms a soft ball that flattens of its own accord when removed. Remove from heat. Pour over pecan mixture. Stir until stiffened. Pour out onto greased baking sheet. Separate into single pieces. Cool completely. Makes 5 cups (1.25 L).

1/2 cup (125 mL): 363 Calories; 23.3 g Total Fat; 7 mg Sodium; 3 g Protein; 40 g Carbohydrate; 2 g Dietary Fiber

Pictured on page 149.

Center Left: Orange Fudgey Pecans, above
Center Right: Curried Almonds, this page
Far Right: Roasted Pecans, above
Bottom: Spiced Nuts, this page

Barbecued Pecans, below

Sugared Nuts, below

Barbecued Pecans

Smoky treats with a kick from the cayenne.

Hard margarine (or butter)	2 tbsp.	30 mL
Worcestershire sauce	2 tbsp.	30 mL
Chili powder	1 tsp.	5 mL
Onion salt	1/4 tsp.	1 mL
Cayenne pepper	1/8-1/4 tsp.	0.5-1 mL
Garlic salt	1/8 tsp.	0.5 mL
Seasoned salt	1/2 tsp.	2 mL
Liquid smoke	1/16 tsp.	0.5 mL
Pecan halves	2 cups	500 mL

Melt margarine in large saucepan. Add next 7 ingredients. Stir.

Add pecans. Toss to coat well. Spread on ungreased 10 x 15 inch (25 x 38 cm) jelly roll pan. Bake in 300°F (150°C) oven for 35 minutes, stirring every 10 minutes. Makes 2 cups (500 mL).

1/2 cup (125 mL): 440 Calories; 44.5 g Total Fat; 428 mg Sodium; 5 g Protein; 12 g Carbohydrate; 4 g Dietary Fiber

Pictured above.

Sugared Nuts

Very tasty—sweet but with just enough savory from the nutmeg, cinnamon and cloves.

Granulated sugar	1/2 cup	125 mL
Salt	1/2 tsp.	2 mL
Ground nutmeg	1/4 tsp.	1 mL
Ground cinnamon	1/4 tsp.	1 mL
Ground cloves	1/8 tsp.	0.5 mL
Egg white (large)	1	1
Unsalted walnuts, pecans and cashews	3 cups	750 mL

Combine all 7 ingredients in large bowl. Stir to coat well. Spread out on greased 11 x 17 inch (28 x 43 cm) baking sheet. Bake in 250°F (120°C) oven for 1 hour. Cool completely. Store in airtight container. Makes 3 cups (750 mL).

1/2 cup (125 mL): 450 Calories; 35 g Total Fat; 213 mg Sodium; 8 g Protein; 32 g Carbohydrate; 3 g Dietary Fiber

Pictured above.

Yam Crisps And Cajun Dip

A delicious change from potato chips. If yams are not available in your local store, use sweet potatoes.

Peeled and thinly sliced yam	2 cups	500 mL
Cooking oil, for deep frying		
CAJUN DIP		
Light mayonnaise (or salad dressing)	1/2 cup	125 mL
Light sour cream	1/2 cup	125 mL
Cajun seasoning	1 tbsp.	15 mL
Lemon juice	1 tsp.	5 mL
Green onion, chopped	1	1

Deep fry yam slices in hot cooking oil for 2 to 3 minutes until golden brown. Remove with slotted spoon to paper towels to drain.

Cajun Dip: Combine all 5 ingredients in small bowl. Let stand for 2 to 3 hours to allow flavors to blend. Makes 1 cup (250 mL).

5 yam crisps with 2 tbsp. (30 mL) dip: 157 Calories; 11.5 g Total Fat; 541 mg Sodium; 1 g Protein; 13 g Carbohydrate; 2 g Dietary Fiber

Pictured below.

Yam Crisps And Cajun Dip, above

Crostini

Golden, crisp and bite size!

Olive (or cooking) oil	1/2 cup	125 mL
Garlic powder	2 tsp.	10 mL
Baguette, cut into 1/4 inch (6 mm) slices	1	1

Combine olive oil and garlic powder in small bowl.

Dab both sides of bread slices with olive oil mixture. Lay out on large baking sheet. Bake in 325°F (160°C) oven for about 25 minutes until golden brown and crispy. Makes about 64 pieces.

1 piece: 33 Calories; 1.9 g Total Fat; 41 mg Sodium; 1 g Protein; 4 g Carbohydrate; trace Dietary Fiber

Pictured on this page.

Bagel Chips

To make these more interesting, use flavored bagels like sesame, multi-grain, sun-dried tomato or cheese.

Large bagels	**3**	**3**

Cut bagels into quarters. Thinly slice each piece. Lay out in single layer or slightly overlapping on baking sheet. Bake in 325°F (160°C) oven for about 15 minutes until golden brown and crisp. Makes about 120 (10 dozen) chips.

1 chip: 6 Calories; 0 g Total Fat; 12 mg Sodium; trace Protein; 1 g Carbohydrate; trace Dietary Fiber

Pictured on page 152/153.

Tortilla Crisps

These are excellent for dipping. Mild chili flavor.

Flour tortillas (10 inch, 25 cm, size)	10	10
Cooking oil	1/3 cup	75 mL
Chili powder	3/4 tsp.	4 mL
Seasoned salt	1/4 tsp.	1 mL

Cut tortillas into 8 wedges each. Place on ungreased baking sheet.

Combine cooking oil, chili powder and seasoned salt in small bowl. Brush one side of each tortilla wedge with cooking oil mixture. Bake in 400°F (205°C) oven for about 7 to 8 minutes. Makes 80 wedges.

1 wedge: 22 Calories; 1.2 g Total Fat; 25 mg Sodium; trace Protein; 2 g Carbohydrate; trace Dietary Fiber

Pictured on page 153.

From left to right:

Crostini, above
Antipasto, page 14
Bagel Chips, above
Veggie Salsa, page 14
Tortilla Crisps, above

Veggie
Salsa

Bon Voyage

Trail Mix, this page

Easy Snack Pack

Lots of shapes and colors in this quick-to-make, easy-to-wrap gift. Double or triple as desired. Fill cellophane gift bags, available at most card shops, and tie with curly ribbon.

Salted peanuts (or cashews or mixed nuts)	1 cup	250 mL
Raisins	1 cup	250 mL
Pecan halves	1 cup	250 mL
Flake coconut	1 cup	250 mL
Chopped dried apricots	1 cup	250 mL
Dried banana slices	1 cup	250 mL
Candy-coated chocolate candies (such as M & M's or Smarties)	1/2 cup	125 mL

Combine all 7 ingredients in large bowl. Toss to coat well. Store in airtight container. Makes 6 1/2 cups (1.6 L).

1/2 cup (125 mL): 287 Calories; 18.2 g Total Fat; 110 mg Sodium; 6 g Protein; 31 g Carbohydrate; 4 g Dietary Fiber

Pictured on front cover.

Trail Mix

Looks just like a commercial Trail Mix. Be sure and try the coating variations too.

Chopped dried apricots	1 cup	250 mL
Golden raisins	1 cup	250 mL
Dark raisins	1 cup	250 mL
Chopped dried pineapple	1 cup	250 mL
Chopped dried pears	1 cup	250 mL
Dried banana slices	1 cup	250 mL
Pecan halves	1 cup	250 mL
Broken cashews	1 cup	250 mL
Peanuts	1 cup	250 mL
Hard margarine (or butter)	1/4 cup	60 mL
Seasoned salt	1 tsp.	5 mL
Salt	2 tsp.	10 mL

Combine first 9 ingredients in large roasting pan.

Melt margarine in small saucepan. Add seasoned salt. Stir. Drizzle over fruit mixture. Stir to coat well.

Sprinkle with salt. Bake, uncovered, in 350°F (175°C) oven for 15 minutes, stirring halfway through. Makes 9 1/2 cups (2.4 L).

1/2 cup (125 mL): 298 Calories; 14.4 g Total Fat; 347 mg Sodium; 5 g Protein; 43 g Carbohydrate; 4 g Dietary Fiber

Pictured on this page.

Variation: For added flavor, add 1 tsp. (5 mL) Worcestershire sauce or 2 tsp. (10 mL) barbecue sauce or 2 tsp. (10 mL) teriyaki sauce to melted margarine.

Gifts for the Home

This section features non-food gift ideas for all ages. Children will enjoy craft kits such as play dough and cookie cutters or finger paints and fun paper. Adults will appreciate bath products and dried herb decorations. We've included instructions on using dough art to make an assortment of decorations, but your imagination can likely come up with many more ideas. Show all your bird-watching friends that you care about their hobby by making edibles to attract wild birds to their yard. And any dog or cat owner will be touched if you remember Fido or Fifi with a delicious treat presented in a new food bowl.

Fruit And Spice Garland, page 156

Fruit Garland

Hang as a strand on your kitchen wall or cupboard,
or drape as a garland in your window.

Large oranges (or tangelos)	1 - 3	1 - 3
Large red Delicious apples	1 - 3	1 - 3
Lemon juice, approximately	1 cup	250 mL

Butchers' string (or jute twine or ribbon)
Darning needle

Cut oranges crosswise into 1/4 inch (6 mm) thick slices. Remove seeds if desired.

Cut whole apples (do not peel or core) crosswise into 1/4 inch (6 mm) thick slices. Brush slices on both sides with lemon juice. Lay orange slices and apple slices in single layer on lightly greased baking sheets. Bake in 200°F (95°C) oven for about 1 hour. Turn slices over. Bake for about 1 1/2 hours until dried but not browned. Cool completely.

Thread string through darning needle. Tie knot in one end. Thread string from front to back at 1 side of apple slice then from back to front at other side of slice, then back to front and front to back through slice of orange. Repeat, alternating slices, until garland is desired length. Knot other end of string.

FRUIT AND SPICE GARLAND: Thread string through holes in hands of Spiced Ornaments, page 157, going from front to back and from back to front, then front to back and back to front through apple slice, then back to front and front to back through orange slice. Repeat until garland is desired length.

Pictured on page 155 and below.

Spiced Ornaments

These ornaments can be used for gift tags,
wall hangings, refrigerator magnets or tree ornaments.
Their spicy aroma is perfect for the kitchen anytime.
Even while drying, the scent will be noticed.

Ground cinnamon	1 cup	250 mL
Ground allspice	1 tbsp.	15 mL
Ground nutmeg	1 tbsp.	15 mL
Fine decorative glitter (optional)	4 tsp.	20 mL
Unsweetened applesauce	3/4 cup	175 mL
White craft glue	2 tbsp.	30 mL

Drinking straw
Butchers' string (or jute twine or ribbon)
Glue gun (optional)
Magnetic strips (optional)

Combine cinnamon, allspice, nutmeg and glitter in medium bowl. Stir in applesauce and glue. Stir, adding more applesauce, 1 tbsp. (15 mL) at a time, as needed to make soft dough. Makes about 1 2/3 cups (400 mL) dough.

Divide dough into smaller portions. Roll out each portion between sheets of waxed paper to 1/4 inch (6 mm) thickness. Cut with cookie cutters into desired shapes. Use a drinking straw to punch a hole (or holes) to thread string for hanging. Place on lightly greased baking sheets. Bake in 200°F (95°C) oven for 30 to 45 minutes until dry. (There is no need to turn at half-time.) Thread with string or glue magnets onto back.

Pictured below.

Photo Legend next page:

1. Dough Art Basket, page 160
2. Dough Art Jar, page 162
3. Dough Art Picture Frame, page 161
4. Dough Art Napkin Rings, page 163
5. Dough Art Fridge Magnets, page 163

3-D Dough

This dough can be used to create refrigerator magnets, lapel pins, napkin holders, baskets and much more. Regular liquid food coloring works well but paste food coloring is easier to use and creates richer colors. Paste food coloring is available at craft and kitchen supply stores.

All-purpose flour	2 cups	500 mL
Salt	2/3 cup	150 mL
Water	3/4 cup	175 mL

Combine flour and salt in large bowl. Gradually stir in water until mixture forms a ball. Turn out onto lightly floured surface. Knead for 3 to 5 minutes until smooth.

Pictured on pages 158 to 163.

How To

Dough Art Basket

Make a pretty container for silk flowers or Easter eggs.

Materials: 1 recipe of 3-D Dough (above), food coloring, rolling pin, pastry cutter, small bowl covered on outside with foil, paring knife, small flower-shaped cookie cutters, small bowl of water, baking sheet, clear glaze, paintbrush.

1. Color 1/2 cup (125 mL) dough green, 1 tsp. (5 mL) dough yellow, 1/4 cup (60 mL) dough each of purple, blue and pink. Leave remaining dough plain.

2. Lightly grease outside of foil. Roll out plain dough to generous 1/4 inch (6 mm) thickness into 8 × 10 inch (20 × 25 cm) rectangle. Cut 8 strips 1 × 7 inches (2.5 × 18 cm) wide. Turn bowl upside down on baking sheet. Place strips over foil. Trim strips at base of bowl to eliminate overlapping so bowl will sit even.

3. Roll colored portions of dough to 1/4 inch (6 mm) thickness. Cut out 8 flowers of purple, blue and pink. Roll tiny balls of yellow dough for flower centers. Wet slightly. Attach to flowers. Cut out 8 green leaves. Roll remaining green dough into 2 long vines 1/2 inch (12 mm) thick. Wet flowers, vines and leaves slightly. Attach to dough basket.

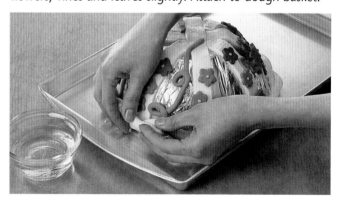

4. Trim dough ends around rim of bowl. Roll remaining dough into two 20 inch (50 cm) ropes. Twist together. Wet slightly. Attach to rim of dough basket. Bake in 300°F (150°C) oven for 45 minutes. Gently turn right side up. Remove bowl and foil. Bake for 15 minutes. Cool. Coat with glaze to protect and seal. See finished basket on page 158.

How To

Dough Art Picture Frame

*This frame offers a stylish way to display
your favorite photograph.*

Materials: 1/2 recipe of 3-D Dough, page 160 (colored 3/4 light green, 1/8 dark green, 1/8 red), rolling pin, pastry cutter, small bowl of water, lightly greased baking sheet (not shown), small round cookie cutter, clear glaze, paintbrush, scissors, cardboard, fabric, iron, glue gun, round 4 × 6 inch (10 × 15 cm) picture.

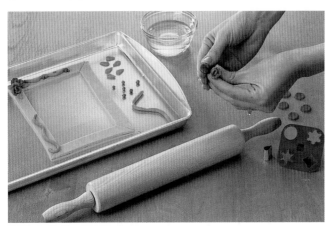

1. Roll light green and red doughs to 1/4 inch (6 mm) thickness. Cut light green dough into 2 strips 1 × 5 inches (2.5 × 12.5 cm) and 2 strips 1 × 7 inches (2.5 × 18 cm). Wet ends slightly with water. Overlap to form rectangle on baking sheet. Cut out red dough into small circles. Shape five small circles around each other into 1 rose. Form vines and leaves out of dark green dough. Wet roses, vines and leaves slightly to attach to frame. Bake in 300°F (150°C) oven for 30 minutes. Cool. Coat with glaze to protect and seal.

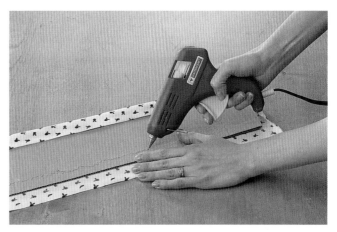

2. Cut cardboard into 4 1/2 × 15 inch (11 × 37 cm) rectangle. Cut fabric into 6 1/2 × 17 inch (16 × 42.5 cm) rectangle. Iron 1/4 inch (6 mm) fold around all edges of fabric. Glue onto cardboard.

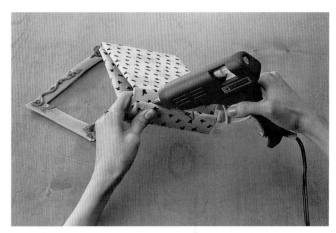

3. Fold cardboard in half. Fold in 1 inch (2.5 cm) from each end. Make tent by overlapping ends and gluing.

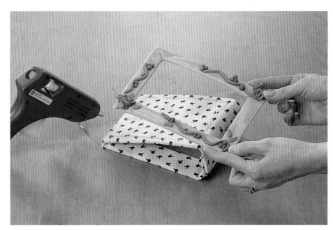

4. Glue sides and bottom of cardboard backing. Attach to frame. Leave top open to slide in picture See finished frame, page 159.

How To

Dough Art Jar

*Turn a plain jar into a conversation piece
to hold cotton balls or candy!*

Materials: 1/2 recipe of 3-D Dough (page 160), rolling pin, jar, paring knife, small bowl of water, fork, wire rack, baking sheet, acrylic paint, paintbrushes, clear glaze.

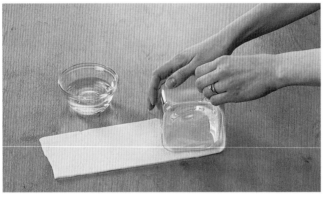

1. Roll 2/3 of dough to 1/4 inch (6 mm) thickness. Cut rectangle long enough to fit completely around jar and wide enough to cover height of jar. Roll out another piece the same size as bottom of jar with remaining dough. Wet dough slightly on one side. Roll around jar, smoothing out air bubbles as you go.

2. Wet bottom piece of dough slightly on one side. Attach to bottom of jar.

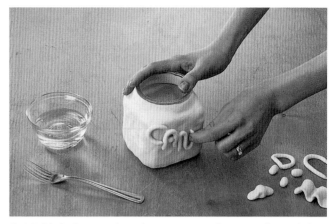

3. Mold designs such as letters or candies out of remaining dough. Wet designs slightly with water to attach. Crimp edge of rim with fork.

4. Place jar upside down on wire rack on baking sheet. Bake in 300°F (150°C) oven for 30 to 45 minutes. Cool.

5. Paint. Dry completely. Coat with glaze to protect and seal. See finished jar on pages 158/159.

How To

Dough Art Napkin Rings

Give a set of napkin rings along with napkins and place mats to personalize the gift. Makes 8 rings.

Materials: 1/2 recipe of 3-D Dough (page 160), 2 toilet paper rolls covered with foil and lightly greased, small bowl of water, lightly greased baking sheet, acrylic paint, paintbrushes, clear glaze.

1. Divide 3/4 of dough into 8 portions. Roll 1 portion into 6 inch (15 cm) rope. Flatten. Wrap around toilet paper roll. Wet ends slightly with water; overlap and press to seal. Repeat with remaining portions, wrapping four rings around each toilet paper roll. Using remaining 1/4 of dough, mold designs. Wet slightly with water to attach to napkin ring. Lay toilet paper rolls on lightly greased baking sheet. Bake in 300°F (150°C) oven for 30 minutes. Cool.

2. Paint. Dry completely. Finish according to recipe, page 160. See finished napkin rings on page 159.

How To

Dough Art Fridge Magnets

Make cute shapes out of dough and turn them into magnets.

Materials: 1/2 recipe of 3-D Dough (page 160), paring knife, paintbrushes, small bowl of water, acrylic paint, self-adhesive magnet, scissors.

1. Shape dough into strawberries (or design of your choice). Take end of paintbrush and dent dough all over on lower part of berry. Roll tiny ovals of dough for seeds. Wet tiny ovals slightly with water to attach to berry. Bake in 300°F (150°C) oven for 30 minutes. Cool. Paint. Dry completely. Coat with glaze to protect and seal. Cut strip of self-adhesive magnet to fit back of berry. Peel off tape. Affix magnet to berry. See finished fridge magnets on pages 158/159.

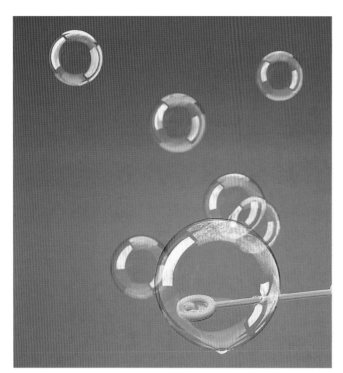

Bubbles, below

Bubbles

Be creative with what you use for bubble wands. For example, the little plastic green basket that strawberries are often packaged in makes tons of bubbles.

Water	2 cups	500 mL
Liquid dish soap (not dishwasher)	1/3 cup	75 mL
Glycerin (available at pharmacy counter)	6 tbsp.	100 mL
Corn syrup	1 tsp.	5 mL
Food coloring (optional)		

Wide-mouthed jar (or other container) with tight-fitting lid
Leftover egg-decorating ladle or bubble wand
Ribbon

Stir first 5 ingredients together in large bowl. Makes 2 1/2 cups (625 mL).

Pour into jar. Attach ladle to outside of jar using ribbon.

Pictured above.

DIRECTIONS FOR

Bubbles: Stir. Dip wand into liquid. Carefully lift out. Hold near mouth and gently blow. Do not use indoors.

How To

Decorative Ice Bowl

Make this ice bowl to chill seafood dip and shrimp when you're invited to a party. It will surprise and delight your host or hostess.

We used seashells in this example, but you could also freeze fruit such as grapes, cherries, slices of orange and peach to go with fruit dip. Cut up pretty starfruit to accent pineapple slices and berries to show off a punch recipe. Freeze salad greens and sliced vegetables to go with vegetable dip. In the summer, freeze flowers in this bowl and give it with a large pillar candle to light up an evening patio party. In the winter, freeze cranberries, mistletoe and evergreen sprigs. Given with a stout candle, your host can sit it outside on a step to welcome guests and it will remain frozen.

Materials: Large bowl that allows approximately 1 inch (2.5 cm) space around a smaller bowl, duct tape, assorted shells, paper doily, platter, floater candles.

1. Fill large bowl with 1 inch (2.5 cm) water. Freeze to form base.

2. Insert small bowl on ice base in large bowl. Secure small bowl in center of large bowl with duct tape.

3. Insert seashells between small and large bowls. Fill with water to within 1 inch (2.5 cm) of rim. Freeze. Remove duct tape. Fill small bowl with lukewarm water to thaw just enough to remove. Set large bowl in sink filled with lukewarm water just long enough to thaw. Remove ice form. Set on doily centered on deep platter. Set small bowl filled with cocktail sauce and shrimp in ice bowl. To transport, keep ice bowl in large bowl until you reach your destination.

4. Place Ice Bowl in deep platter (see finished bowl below). Once ice has melted, remove doily and any other wilted garnishes. Set 2 or 3 floater candles in remaining water. Light and enjoy the end-of-a-nice-evening ambiance it creates.

Decorative Ice Bowl, page 164

Spicy Sachet

Here's a wonderful fragrance to fill your home—simply double or triple the recipe and make as many bags as you wish.

Cinnamon sticks (about 7 inches, 18 cm, each)	4	4
Plastic bag		
Meat mallet		
Whole nutmeg	2	2
Dark espresso coffee beans	10	10
Whole allspice	6	6
Whole cloves	10	10
Light cotton fabric		
Pinking shears (optional)		
Elastic band	1	1
Ribbon, for tying		

Place cinnamon sticks in plastic bag. Using mallet, break and slightly crush cinnamon sticks. Empty into small bowl.

Repeat with nutmeg and coffee beans. Empty into bowl.

Repeat with allspice and cloves. Empty into bowl. Makes 1/3 cup (75 mL) spice mix.

Cut 10 inch (25 cm) square or circle of fabric using pinking shears. Turn out spice mix into center of square. Gather up corners of fabric and close with elastic band. Pull up on ends to tighten slightly. Tie with pretty ribbon.

Pictured on back cover.

DIRECTIONS FOR

Spicy Sachet: Suspend this sachet under the hood fan over your stove and enjoy the fragrance anytime you're cooking. Moist heat allows the spices to release their scent. Scent will last for many weeks.

Aromatic Mix, this page

Aromatic Mix

Make as much of this recipe as you like for family and friends.

Cinnamon sticks (about 4 inches, 10 cm, each), broken up	2	2
Mixed pickling spice	1 1/2 tbsp.	25 mL
Whole cloves	20	20
Whole allspice, coarsely cracked	1 tsp.	5 mL

Combine all 4 ingredients in resealable plastic bag. Makes about 1/2 cup (125 mL).

Pictured below.

Holiday Aromatic

What a lovely gift for a Christmas open house or holiday host.

Cinnamon sticks (about 4 inches, 10 cm, each), broken up	3	3
Whole cloves	3 tbsp.	50 mL
Dried lemon peel	1 tbsp.	15 mL
Dried orange bits	1 tsp.	5 mL

Combine all 4 ingredients in resealable plastic bag. Makes about 1/2 cup (125 mL).

Pictured below.

DIRECTIONS FOR

Aromatic Mix and Holiday Aromatic: Empty contents of bag into 4 cups (1 L) simmering water in large saucepan. Stir. Simmer, uncovered, for as long as aroma is desired. Cool. Refrigerate to use again.

Holiday Aromatic, above

Play Dough

Whether you know a stay-at-home mom who could use a new activity for her child or a sick child looking for a quiet way to pass the time, play dough is the answer.

Water	2 1/2 cups	625 mL
Drops of food coloring	8	8
Salt	1 cup	250 mL
All-purpose flour	2 cups	500 mL
Cooking oil	2 tbsp.	30 mL
Cream of tartar	2 tbsp.	30 mL

Combine water and food coloring in large saucepan to get an even color.

Add remaining 4 ingredients. Heat and stir until mixture forms a soft ball. Remove from heat. Cool for 5 minutes. Turn out onto counter. Knead until smooth. Place in airtight plastic container for gift-giving. Makes about 4 cups (1 L).

Pictured on page 168 and page 169.

DIRECTIONS FOR

Play Dough: Store in plastic container or resealable plastic bag in refrigerator for up to 4 weeks. Children should be supervised while playing with Play Dough. Not to be eaten!

Yummy Play Dough

This dough works well for those little ones who insist on eating the dough or licking their fingers. You will still want to supervise how much is being eaten to avoid sore tummies!

Container of prepared white frosting	16 oz.	450 g
Smooth peanut butter	1 cup	250 mL
Icing (confectioner's) sugar	1 1/2 cups	375 mL
Food coloring		

Beat frosting and peanut butter in large bowl until blended.

Gradually knead in icing sugar until very stiff. Knead in food coloring. Knead in additional icing sugar if dough is sticky. Place in airtight plastic container for gift-giving. Makes 3 cups (750 mL).

Pictured on page 169.

DIRECTIONS FOR

Yummy Play Dough: Store in plastic container or resealable plastic bag in refrigerator for up to 4 weeks. Safe for children. Caution: Contains peanut butter.

Smelly Play Dough

Not edible, but it sure smells good!

All-purpose flour	1 cup	250 mL
Salt	1/2 cup	125 mL
Package of unsweetened fruit-flavored drink mix	1/4 oz.	8 g
Cream of tartar	2 tsp.	10 mL
Water	1 cup	250 mL
Cooking oil	1 tbsp.	15 mL

Combine flour, salt, drink mix and cream of tartar in medium saucepan. Stir in water and cooking oil. Heat and stir until thickened. (Consistency should resemble mashed potatoes.) Remove from heat. Cool for 5 minutes. Turn out onto lightly floured surface. Knead until dry but pliable. Cool completely. Place in airtight plastic container for gift-giving. Makes 2 cups (500 mL).

Pictured on page 168 and page 169.

DIRECTIONS FOR

Smelly Play Dough: Store in plastic container or resealable plastic bag in refrigerator for up to 4 weeks. Children should be supervised when playing with Smelly Play Dough. Not to be eaten!

Photo Legend next page:

1. Smelly Play Dough, above
2. Yummy Play Dough, this page
3. Play Dough, this page

Happy Birthday
Nicholas

Rainy-Day Paint

Carve a raised potato design and brush with some of this paint. Stamp design onto homemade wrapping such as inside-out cereal boxes or brown paper. Or package the pretty jars of paint in a plastic pail with wide brushes and blank paper. It's fun and economical.

Cold water	1 1/2 cups	375 mL
All-purpose flour	1/3 cup	75 mL
Cold water	1 tbsp.	15 mL
Liquid dish soap	1 tbsp.	15 mL
Small jars with tight-fitting lids (1/2 cup, 125 mL, each)	4	4
Paste food coloring (not regular), see Note		

Stir first amount of cold water into flour in small saucepan until smooth. Heat and stir until thickened. Remove from heat.

Press a large piece of plastic wrap over surface of liquid. Cool to lukewarm. Remove plastic wrap. Whisk in second amount of cold water and liquid soap until smooth.

Divide mixture among jars. Stir food coloring into mixture, a little at a time, to desired colors. Makes 1 2/3 cups (400 mL), enough for 4 different colors.

Pictured on page 171.

Note: Paste food coloring is available at craft and kitchen supply stores. It is less messy to use and creates brighter colors.

DIRECTIONS FOR

Rainy-Day Paint: Store in refrigerator for up to 3 days.

Shiny Finger Paint

This paint can be used on any kind of paper and will have a slight shine to it once it dries.

Envelope of unflavored gelatin	1/4 oz.	7 g
Cold water	1/4 cup	60 mL
Cornstarch	1/2 cup	125 mL
Cold water	3 cups	750 mL
Small jars with tight-fitting lids (1/2 cup, 125 mL, each)	4 - 6	4 - 6
Paste food coloring (not regular), see Note		

Combine gelatin and first amount of cold water in small bowl. Let stand for about 5 minutes to soften gelatin.

Combine cornstarch and second amount of cold water in medium saucepan. Heat and stir until boiling and thickened. Stir in gelatin until dissolved.

Divide gelatin mixture among jars. Stir food coloring into mixture, a little at a time, to desired colors. Makes about 3 cups (750 mL), enough for 6 different colors.

Pictured on page 171.

Note: Paste food coloring is available at craft and kitchen supply stores. It is less messy to use and creates brighter colors.

DIRECTIONS FOR

Shiny Finger Paint: Store in refrigerator for up to 3 days.

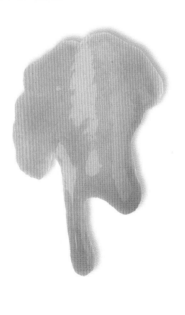

Left: Shiny Finger Paint, above
Right: Rainy-Day Paint, this page

Rainy
Day
Survival
Kit

Air Freshener

Depending on the scent used, this can be a mild or strong air freshener. Adding food coloring will produce a layered effect.

Distilled water	3 cups	750 mL
Envelopes of unflavored gelatin (1/4 oz., 7 g, each)	6	6
Salt	3 tbsp.	50 mL
Fragrance oil (use more or less as desired)	1/2 tsp.	2 mL
Food coloring (optional)		
Small decorative, wide-mouthed jars with tight-fitting lids	1 - 4	1 - 4

Combine distilled water and gelatin in large saucepan. Let stand for 10 minutes to soften gelatin. Heat and stir on medium for 1 minute. Add salt. Heat and stir to dissolve gelatin and salt. Remove from heat. Cool for 30 minutes.

Stir in fragrance oil and food coloring to desired color.

Pour into small decorative jars. Let stand at room temperature for about 1 hour until solid. Makes 3 cups (750 mL).

Pictured on page 173.

Marbled Stone Scents

Use these lightly scented stones as a base to hold dried flowers in a pretty vase. The scent will last for several months.

All-purpose flour	3/4 cup	175 mL
Salt	3/4 cup	175 mL
Boiling water	3/4 cup	175 mL
Fragrance oil (use more or less as desired)	2 tsp.	10 mL
Food coloring		

Combine flour and salt in medium bowl. Make a well in center.

Pour boiling water and fragrance oil into well. Stir. Scent will be strong but does fade while drying.

Knead in food coloring without overworking until a marbled effect is created. With dampened hands, shape dough into irregular-shaped stones. Place on greased baking sheet. Bake in 200°F (95°C) oven, with oven door slightly open, for 2 to 2 1/2 hours, turning after 1 hour, until hardened. Makes about 23 stones.

Pictured on page 173.

Bath Bombs

The baking soda and citric acid produce a gentle fizzing.

Baking soda	1 1/2 cups	375 mL
Citric acid (available at pharmacy counter)	1/2 cup	125 mL
Fragrance oil (use more or less as desired)	1 1/2 tsp.	7 mL
Food coloring		
Water, in a spray bottle		
Small scoop (or hard plastic candy molds)		

Combine baking soda and citric acid in small bowl.

Add fragrance oil and food coloring. Mix well. Spray surface of mixture with water until dampened. Mix well. Keep spraying and mixing until mixture just begins to clump. Makes 2 cups (500 mL).

Form balls with hands or scoop into balls or press firmly into molds. Release onto waxed paper-lined baking sheets. Allow to dry at room temperature for about 8 hours.

Pictured on page 173.

DIRECTIONS FOR

Bath Bomb: As with any product, anyone with sensitive skin should test this product first before bathing. Fill bathtub with water. Add bath bomb. Submerse arm for five minutes. Check for reaction.

Milk Bath In A Jar

These scented crystals will leave skin feeling soft.

Skim milk powder	2 cups	500 mL
Baking soda	1/2 cup	125 mL
Cornstarch	1 tbsp.	15 mL
Fragrance oil (use more or less as desired)	1/2 tsp.	2 mL

Process first 3 ingredients in food processor until powdery.

Pour mixture into resealable plastic bag or container with tight-fitting lid. Add fragrance oil. Shake well to distribute oil.

Pictured on page 173.

DIRECTIONS FOR

Milk Bath In A Jar: Pour 1/2 cup (125 mL) crystals under warm, running water in bathtub. Scent will last for about 15 minutes.

Center Left: Air Freshener, this page
Centre: Milk Bath In A Jar, above
Center Right: Marbled Stone Scents, this page
Bottom: Bath Bombs, above

Milk Bath

Take a Break

How To

Drying Herbs

Dried herbs can be used for cooking or for decorating. If you grow herbs in your garden, you can make the following decorations at a fraction of the cost of purchasing them! Good herbs for decorating are anise, basil, bay, dill, lavender, mint, parsley, rosemary, sage, tarragon, thyme. You can also dry various types of chili peppers using this same method.

1. Harvest herb leaves in the morning, when the first flower buds appear, to get the most flavor and fragrance. To encourage annual plants to keep growing, leave four to six inches (10-15 cm) of the stem. For perennial herbs, cut only one-third of the plant at a time.

2. Clean the leaves under cool running water, then allow to air dry on paper towels. Gather 6 stems together and tie in a bundle with string or elastic band. Hang upside down and allow to dry for up to 14 days. Humidity in different parts of the country will affect drying time.

3. Lay small leaf herbs on a cooling rack to dry. Alternatively, use a piece of screen stapled over some 1 × 1 inch (2.5 × 2.5 cm) lumber to form a rack. You can also dry herbs in an oven on baking sheets at the lowest temperature, usually 150°F to 175°F (65°C to 80°C), for 3 or 4 hours with the door open. To prevent mold, ensure that the leaves are thoroughly dried.

4. To use the herbs for cooking, remove leaves from stems. Crush. Store in airtight jars in a cool, dry place.

Top: Herb Wreath, page 176
Center: Herb Swag, page 176
Bottom: Herb Hat, page 177

Herb Swag

This pretty, dried herb swag will look attractive over a window or door (shown on page 174/175). Swag forms and florist foam, also called oasis, are available at craft stores.

Materials: Florist foam, swag form, scissors, glue gun, dried moss, floral pins, ribbon, wire, wire cutters, florist tape, assorted dried herbs and fruit.

1. Cut florist foam to fit center of swag form. Attach with glue. Pin moss to foam with floral pins.

2. Make bow (see page 12) with ribbon, wire and wire cutters. Secure by poking wire into foam.

3. Wrap ends of dried herbs with florist tape to strengthen. Arrange by poking large leaf herbs into foam first, followed by small leaf herbs.

4. Thread wire through dried fruit. Push wire into foam.

Herb Wreath

An herb wreath looks great hanging from an entry door to welcome guests or from a curtain rod to dress up a window (shown on page 175).

Materials: Ribbon (at least 36 inches, 1 m, depending on width), glue gun, wreath form, scissors, wire, wire cutters, assorted dried herbs and dried chili peppers.

1. Glue end of ribbon to wreath. Wrap ribbon snugly around wreath form. Cut to match first end. Glue to secure.

2. Make bow (see page 12) with remaining ribbon, wire and wire cutters. Secure by tying wire around wreath form where ribbon ends meet.

3. Glue large herbs leaves in place, followed by small herb leaves and chili peppers.

How To

Herb Hat

Use Spicy Sachet ingredients, page 166, in this novel way to create a beautiful wall decoration.

Materials: Hat form, Spicy Sachet ingredients, muslin, scissors, needle, thread to match hat color, ribbon, dried herbs, cinnamon sticks, embellishments.

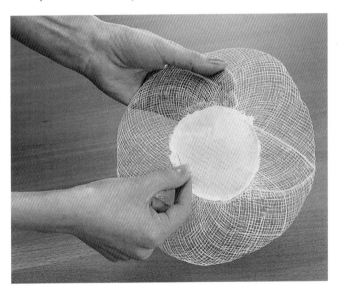

1. Fill crown of hat with Spicy Sachet ingredients. Cut piece of muslin 1 inch (2.5 cm) larger in diameter than crown opening. Hold muslin over crown opening. Hand stitch in place. Decorate hat brim with ribbon, dried herbs, cinnamon sticks and embellishments (shown on page 174/175).

Bird Breakfast

Feathered friends will enjoy these patties in the morning and throughout the day. These will last particularly well outdoors in cold weather, placed in a suet holder or on a flat surfaced bird feeder.

Quick-cooking rolled oats (not instant)	1 1/2 cups	375 mL
Boiling water	2 cups	500 mL
Chunky peanut butter (no salt, no sugar)	1/2 cup	125 mL
Suet (or vegetable shortening)	3/4 cup	175 mL
Commercial birdseed	1/2 cup	125 mL
Yellow cornmeal	1 cup	250 mL
Cream of wheat cereal (not instant)	1 cup	250 mL
Chopped dried cranberries	1/3 cup	75 mL

Cook rolled oats in boiling water in large saucepan for about 2 minutes, stirring constantly, until very thick. Remove from heat.

Stir in peanut butter and suet until melted. Stir in remaining 4 ingredients. Cool enough to handle. Shape into large patties. Place on ungreased baking sheet. Freeze until hard. Place in resealable freezer bag. Remove as needed. Makes 4 1/2 cups (1.1 L), enough for about 14 patties.

Pictured below.

Bird Breakfast, above   Bird Feed Treats, page 178

Bird Feed Treats

Save the mesh bags from onions, lemons, limes or tomatoes-on-the-vine to fill with this bird treat.

Dry bread crumbs	2 cups	500 mL
Commercial birdseed	1 cup	250 mL
Chopped unsalted peanuts	1 cup	250 mL
Chopped raisins	1 cup	250 mL
Whole wheat flour	1/2 cup	125 mL
Yellow cornmeal	1/4 cup	60 mL
Cream of wheat cereal (not instant)	1/4 cup	60 mL
Chunky peanut butter (no salt, no sugar)	1 cup	250 mL
Suet (or vegetable shortening)	1 cup	250 mL
Bacon drippings	2 tbsp.	30 mL
Mesh bags	12	12
Butchers' string (or jute twine)		

Combine first 7 ingredients in large bowl.

Heat peanut butter, suet and bacon drippings in small saucepan on medium, stirring occasionally, until melted. Gradually stir into birdseed mixture until moistened. Pack mixture into ice cube trays. Chill well or freeze.

Fill mesh bag with up to 10 cubes. Close. Tie with string. Hang from sturdy branch. Makes about 4 dozen cubes.

Pictured on page 177.

Variation: If you don't have a mesh bag, place a few cubes on a deck or fence rail or on a bird feeder platform.

Bird Feed Cones

Use a higher proportion of black sunflower seeds to attract pretty Blue Jays.

Ribbon, string or yarn, for hanging		
Large pine cones (about 5 inches, 12.5 cm, high)	5 - 6	5 - 6
Chunky peanut butter (no salt, no sugar)	1 cup	250 mL
Vegetable shortening (or bacon or beef drippings)	1/2 cup	125 mL
Yellow cornmeal	1/2 cup	125 mL
Commercial birdseed	1 1/2 cups	375 mL

Tie ribbon to pine cone at bottom (narrow, pointy end). Cut ribbon to desired length.

Melt peanut butter and shortening in small saucepan. Add cornmeal. Heat and stir for 3 to 4 minutes until well mixed.

Transfer cornmeal mixture to shallow pie plate. Roll pine cone in warm mixture, using a rubber spatula, if necessary, to gently spread mixture over and in between "petals" of cones. Place birdseed in deep bowl. Holding pine cone in bowl, spoon birdseed over top, pushing with tip of spoon into cornmeal mixture. Chill on waxed paper-lined baking sheet. Can be frozen. Hang from sturdy branch in summer or winter.

Pictured above.

Left: Canine Cookies, page 180
Right: Fido Biscuits, page 180

Fido Biscuits

Dogs will love these! Attach the recipe and cookie cutter to complete the gift.

All-purpose flour	1 cup	250 mL
Whole wheat flour	1 cup	250 mL
Cooking oil	3 tbsp.	50 mL
Instant rolled oats	2 tbsp.	30 mL
Garlic powder	1 tsp.	5 mL
Water	2/3 cup	150 mL
Beef bouillon powder	1 tsp.	5 mL
Water (optional)	1 1/2 tsp.	7 mL
Gravy browner (optional)	1 tsp.	5 mL

Combine first 7 ingredients in large bowl until dough forms. Turn out onto lightly floured surface. Roll out to 1/4 inch (6 mm) thickness. Cut out with bone-shaped or dog-shaped cookie cutters. Place on ungreased baking sheet. Bake in 375°F (190°C) oven for about 15 minutes.

Combine second amount of water and gravy browner in small cup. Turn biscuits over. Brush with gravy browner mixture. Bake for 10 minutes until browned. Makes about 2 dozen biscuits.

Pictured on page 179.

Canine Cookies

These are quick to make. A great one-a-day treat. Send a new batch every month anonymously to an elderly friend's pet.

Whole wheat flour	1 1/2 cups	375 mL
All-purpose flour	1 cup	250 mL
Skim milk powder	1 cup	250 mL
Melted beef fat (or bacon drippings)	1/3 cup	75 mL
Large egg, fork-beaten	1	1
Cold water	1 cup	250 mL

Combine both flours and milk powder in large bowl. Drizzle with fat. Add egg and cold water. Mix well to form dough. Turn out onto lightly floured surface. Roll out to 1/2 inch (12 mm) thickness. Cut out with bone-shaped or dog-shaped cookie cutters. Place on ungreased baking sheet. Bake in 300°F (150°C) oven for 60 minutes. Makes about 3 dozen cookies.

Pictured on page 179.

Kitty Cat Treats

Kitties deserve presents too!

Whole wheat flour	3/4 cup	175 mL
Skim milk powder	1/4 cup	60 mL
Soy flour (see Note)	2 tbsp.	30 mL
Wheat germ	1 tbsp.	15 mL
Catnip	1/2 tsp.	2 mL
Large egg, fork-beaten	1	1
Cod liver oil	2 tbsp.	30 mL
Water	1/4 cup	60 mL

Combine first 5 ingredients in medium bowl.

Beat 1/2 of egg, cod liver oil and water in small bowl. Add to flour mixture. Mix very well, adding a bit more flour if dough is sticky. Roll pieces of dough on lightly floured surface into long ropes about 1/4 inch (6 mm) in diameter. Cut into 1/4 inch (6 mm) pieces. Repeat with remaining dough. Place pieces on ungreased baking sheet. Bake in 350°F (175°C) oven for 15 minutes. Brush with remaining 1/2 of egg. Bake for 2 minutes. Makes about 180 pieces.

Pictured on page 181.

Note: Soy flour is available in bulk sections of large chain grocery stores or health food stores.

Variation: Roll out dough on lightly floured surface to 1/4 inch (6 mm) thickness. Cut out shapes using tiny cookie cutters. Bake as above. Makes about 260 pieces.

Kitty Cat Treats, page 180

Pet Celebration Cake, this page

Pet Celebration Cake

Even dogs and cats have birthdays! Take this as a gift for a special four-legged friend. Or invite the neighborhood pets over for a shared treat.

Whole wheat flour	1 1/2 cups	375 mL
Baking powder	1 1/2 tsp.	7 mL
Cooking oil	1/2 cup	125 mL
Coarse liverwurst	1/2 cup	125 mL
Jar of strained beef (or veal), with broth (baby food)	4 1/2 oz.	128 mL
Large eggs	4	4
Beef jerky snack for dogs, broken up into small pieces	4	4
Process cheese slices, for garnish		

Combine flour and baking powder in large bowl. Set aside.

Beat cooking oil, liverwurst, strained beef with broth and eggs together in medium bowl until smooth.

Fold in beef jerky snack. Add to flour mixture. Stir. Spread batter in greased foil-lined 8 inch (20 cm) round pan. Bake in 325°F (160°C) oven for about 50 minutes until cooked. Cool. Turn out onto serving platter.

Cut pet's name out of cheese slices. Arrange on top of cake.

Pictured above.

Measurement Tables

Throughout this book measurements are given in Conventional and Metric measure. To compensate for differences between the two measurements due to rounding, a full metric measure is not always used. The cup used is the standard 8 fluid ounce. Temperature is given in degrees Fahrenheit and Celsius. Baking pan measurements are in inches and centimetres as well as quarts and litres. An exact metric conversion is given on this page as well as the working equivalent (Metric Standard Measure).

Oven Temperatures

Fahrenheit (°F)	Celsius (°C)	Fahrenheit (°F)	Celsius (°C)
175°	80°	350°	175°
200°	95°	375°	190°
225°	110°	400°	205°
250°	120°	425°	220°
275°	140°	450°	230°
300°	150°	475°	240°
325°	160°	500°	260°

Spoons

Conventional Measure	Metric Exact Conversion Millilitre (mL)	Metric Standard Measure Millilitre (mL)
1/8 teaspoon (tsp.)	0.6 mL	0.5 mL
1/4 teaspoon (tsp.)	1.2 mL	1 mL
1/2 teaspoon (tsp.)	2.4 mL	2 mL
1 teaspoon (tsp.)	4.7 mL	5 mL
2 teaspoons (tsp.)	9.4 mL	10 mL
1 tablespoon (tbsp.)	14.2 mL	15 mL

Cups

1/4 cup (4 tbsp.)	56.8 mL	60 mL
1/3 cup (5 1/3 tbsp.)	75.6 mL	75 mL
1/2 cup (8 tbsp.)	113.7 mL	125 mL
2/3 cup (10 2/3 tbsp.)	151.2 mL	150 mL
3/4 cup (12 tbsp.)	170.5 mL	175 mL
1 cup (16 tbsp.)	227.3 mL	250 mL
4 1/2 cups	1022.9 mL	1000 mL (1 L)

Pans

Conventional Inches	Metric Centimetres
8 × 8 inch	20 × 20 cm
9 × 9 inch	22 × 22 cm
9 × 13 inch	22 × 33 cm
10 × 15 inch	25 × 38 cm
11 × 17 inch	28 × 43 cm
8 × 2 inch round	20 × 5 cm
9 × 2 inch round	22 × 5 cm
10 × 4 1/2 inch tube	25 × 11 cm
8 × 4 × 3 inch loaf	20 × 10 × 7.5 cm
9 × 5 × 3 inch loaf	22 × 12.5 × 7.5 cm

Dry Measurements

Conventional Measure Ounces (oz.)	Metric Exact Conversion Grams (g)	Metric Standard Measure Grams (g)
1 oz.	28.3 g	28 g
2 oz.	56.7 g	57 g
3 oz.	85.0 g	85 g
4 oz.	113.4 g	125 g
5 oz.	141.7 g	140 g
6 oz.	170.1 g	170 g
7 oz.	198.4 g	200 g
8 oz.	226.8 g	250 g
16 oz.	453.6 g	500 g
32 oz.	907.2 g	1000 g (1 kg)

Casseroles

Canada & Britain

Standard Size Casserole	Exact Metric Measure
1 qt. (5 cups)	1.13 L
1 1/2 qts. (7 1/2 cups)	1.69 L
2 qts. (10 cups)	2.25 L
2 1/2 qts. (12 1/2 cups)	2.81 L
3 qts. (15 cups)	3.38 L
4 qts. (20 cups)	4.5 L
5 qts. (25 cups)	5.63 L

United States

Standard Size Casserole	Exact Metric Measure
1 qt. (4 cups)	900 mL
1 1/2 qts. (6 cups)	1.35 L
2 qts. (8 cups)	1.8 L
2 1/2 qts. (10 cups)	2.25 L
3 qts. (12 cups)	2.7 L
4 qts. (16 cups)	3.6 L
5 qts. (20 cups)	4.5 L

How-To Index

Tip Index

Recipe Index